1012799213
796.5 HOD
HODGSON, MICHAEL
WILDERNESS WITH CHILDREN
: A PARENT'S GUIDE TO FUN
FAMILY OUTINGS   CLINTON
9/93

Date Due

FEB - 6 1996			

Wilderness with Children

A PARENT'S GUIDE
TO FUN FAMILY OUTINGS

Michael Hodgson

STACKPOLE BOOKS

Published by
STACKPOLE BOOKS
Cameron and Kelker Streets
P.O. Box 1831 Harrisburg, PA 17105

Printed in the United States of America

10 9 8 7 6 5 4 3 2

First edition

All photos by the author unless otherwise credited
Cover photo by James Ward
Cover design by Tracy Patterson
Illustrations by Michelle LaGory
Typesetting and mechanical production by ART UNLIMITED

Library of Congress Cataloging-in-Publication Data

Hodgson, Michael.
    Wilderness with children : a parent's guide to fun family outings
  / Michael Hodgson. — 1st ed.
      p.   cm.
    ISBN 0-8117-2416-6
    1. Outdoor recreation for children.   2. Family recreation.
I. Title
GV191.63.H64   1992   91-32071
796.5--dc20   CIP

To my daughter, Nikki, who has patiently shown me a new and wonderful world through the eyes of a child. To my wife, Karen, who sacrifices her time to make room for my crazy schedule, and who lovingly edits everything I write.

Contents

Introduction

PERHAPS IT IS A natural curiosity for things furry, fuzzy, and new; perhaps it is the desire to discover wide-open spaces, to frolic, to tumble, and to hide; or perhaps it is the pull of an unknown spirit. Whatever it is, nature and children go together like peanut butter and jelly.

Take one look at the wide-eyed expression of a little girl who has just blown with all her might on a milkweed and can hardly believe the white fluffy explosion she has caused, and you start to understand the need for sharing the outdoors with children. The outdoors urges discovery and learning—it doesn't allow for less. Nature and outdoors provide personal inspiration like nothing else can. Every minute becomes an individual expression of wonder, delight, and enlightenment.

You don't have to be a descendant of John Muir or Henry Thoreau to pass along the joys of being outdoors to your children. Sharing the outdoors by hiking, camping, or canoeing depends only on your patience and sense of fun. Expect to learn as much from the outdoors through your children as they do through you; after all, nature is the grand instructor and you are merely the facilitator.

"But children are difficult to teach." "They are too young to appreciate camping." "They will never enjoy being away from the television for more than one night." "They will get too tired." "They . . ." I have heard all the excuses. Parents seem to find more and more reasons not to experience the wilderness with their children because they don't have the patience to try. Believe me, taking your kids hiking or camping doesn't require much effort as long as you keep one rule in mind: See everything through a child's eyes.

Children want to be involved, even the youngest ones, with planning, packing, carrying, and guiding. It is very obvious to them when they are considered extra baggage, just "in the way." If you want your children to learn about the outdoors and to enjoy every minute in the sun, then the learning must start at home at the very inception of the activity and last through its completion.

It is true that you will not be able to camp as freely as you once did; you can't pick up at a moment's notice, hike for miles, or gaze silently at nothing in particular for hours. Look at it this way, however: You never could have camped with the same opportunity you have now—seeing everything through the inquisitive, yearning, searching, and undeniably joyful eyes of your child.

You will understand soon, if you do not already, that experiencing nature in the uninhibited manner of children is by far the best way to see it. It doesn't matter how far or how much, how high or how difficult, just as long as there is discovery and fun along the way. Prepare your parental ego for the shock that perhaps your child will be more interested in running around a meadow chasing butterflies than in climbing the "incredible" peak that you had planned. Then, instead of fretting, you will be able to join in your child's simple joy.

When I look back upon my days as a youngster, I remember most vividly those moments spent wandering in the mountains of western Canada and northern Colorado with my mother and father. We never went camping (I went to summer camp for that), but every Sunday was mine to hike and explore. Mine to feed the chipmunks with my mother, scramble through rock fields with my father, or munch wild berries along the trail. My parents were wonderful in not dictating their needs to me; instead they allowed my inquisitiveness to lead us all on. It is with that same outlook that I share the wilds with my own daughter, who is now eight. She takes great pride "helping" Daddy up the steep hills and deciding when to have a snack and where to explore next. I find, through Nikki, that my own sense of discovery and joy for the outdoors is heightened.

Nikki began camping when she was one month old. From those early moments beside a campfire under glittering stars, Nikki's love for being in the mountains has grown. Every family and every situation is unique. Not all parents are going to take their children camping, and certainly not at the age of one month. The outdoors, however, offers each child a special opportunity. I encourage everyone to use and learn from the wilds all that you can. Bask in the simplicity, the wonder, the enlightenment, the sheer joy of being one with the world. I do not think you or your children will be disappointed.

CHAPTER 1

Getting Started

THERE IS A STARTING POINT to everything; so it is with sharing the outdoors with children. Take heed, however, that the failing point to a successful beginning between parents and children is often found in their first outdoor experiences together. Starting with a parent's grandiose idea to climb a favorite peak and camp in a remote and secluded spot that the parent remembers as special is suspect and destined for trouble.

Although I started taking Nikki camping before she was a year old (she had no say in the matter), I planned short excursions. We stayed close to home in warm valleys with nearby meadows for crawling and simple exploring. Keeping it simple and remembering that this is all new to a child is key to success in this adventure. Children do not need high peaks, spectacular views, raging rapids—think about it, you probably didn't start with high demands either.

Children will find joy in clouds, flowers, crawfish hunting, splashing, rolling down a grassy knoll, watching a multicolored bug, or playing one of a hundred nature discovery games with you. It is not fun to be cold, sunburned, hungry, thirsty, exhausted, or frustrated. Keep your first outings simple and fun, and you will discover excitement and adventure through a child's eyes.

The question I'm most often asked is this: At what age is a child old enough to begin hiking and camping? Quite frankly, that depends on your child because there are no hard and fast rules. Some generally acknowledged guidelines, however, should be considered. The following will help you in deciding where and when to begin, but remember that the only firm guide is each child's particular personality and physical condition. Whatever the activity, you must let them pace themselves.

Pediatricians recommend that parents wait until the child is five months of age before venturing out. This is when a child can easily sit up and support his or her own weight and has fallen into a fairly regular sleep pattern. Use a sturdy child carrier that is safe and secure for the child and comfortable for you.

Between the ages of two and four, children are still getting used to the idea of being on two points of balance and not four. Short hikes between one-half and two miles are ideal as long as the terrain is flat and secure to walk on. You will get an idea of your child's attention span by taking regular walks in a neighborhood park. Expect a focused attention of around ten minutes for the young child and up to thirty minutes for older children.

Longer hikes at an easy pace over easy terrain are possible when children are between five and nine years old. Children are beginning to develop more physical and mental durability. This is an ideal age to allow your child to become involved in most aspects of the trip—planning, packing, helping lead, and so on. The older your child is in this age group, the more likely moderate goal setting will be effective. Once again, these must be shared goals and not an unrealistic attempt on the parent's part to motivate a child up an impossible hill or over a ten-mile death march.

At ages ten to thirteen, children are becoming increasingly conditioned physically. Emotionally they are more likely to be able to handle moderately challenging situations, but they are also more likely to question the worth of anything extremely difficult. Hikes up to ten miles are possible. Children in this age group thrive on being the leader, so diplomatic and judicious support from the parent is key. Menu planning, route finding, cooking, and setting up camp are reasonable tasks, but be careful that they do not take on too much and begin to feel like all they are doing is working.

Distances up to twelve miles become reasonable in the fourteen- to eighteen-year-old range. Terrain choices and goal setting can become more challenging, but the axiom remains the same—any choice must be a group one or the parent risks the children feeling "dragged" along. Important to remember is that children are encountering "growth spurts" during this period and are very vulnerable to stress and overuse injuries. Use caution and listen to your children; they may need to take a long break or cut short a hike.

Guidelines and rules aside, the choice of what to do rests with you and your family. No two personalities are the same, no two children the same.

Until she is old enough to walk herself, McKenna will enjoy the woods from her reserved seat on Dad's back.

What may work for my family may not work for yours. Flexibility and adaptability need to be added to your growing arsenal of outdoor camping techniques.

No matter how old your children or how experienced you may be in the outdoors, if any of your family has yet to spend his first minute in the wilderness, then you would be wise to proceed slowly. The foundation for strong wilderness experience must be laid carefully. Plan simple day-trips to local parks and wilderness preserves. Just walking outdoors, drinking from a canteen, carrying a day pack, wearing hiking boots, and eating trail food will all be new to your family.

On your first day-trip you will have much to do and consider. Do your family members have the right clothes? Do their shoes and packs fit? Did everyone bring plenty of water? How about snacks and a trail lunch? Does everyone have rain gear—just in case? Who is carrying the first-aid kit, and who knows how to use it? Is the hike well suited to the abilities of all the participants? How is the walking pace?

Even though you must assume leadership, because of your experience, it is important to remember that this is supposed to be fun and relaxing. So relax and enjoy yourself. Involve everyone in the process. Don't be the only one running around frantically trying to make sure everything is accomplished. Assign responsibilities. Put someone in charge of the first-aid kit. Designate a cook—even though this will be a sack lunch—to plan and pack the meal. Get everyone involved in checking gear and making sure the day packs are appropriately loaded, no one carrying too much or too little.

Make everything in the pack count. Extra weight is not worth it. Children want to and should participate, even the youngest ones. Nikki was carrying a small pack when she was just three. Granted, all she carried was her teddy bear and a box of juice, but it was important for her to feel involved, and quite frankly, for Nikki the teddy bear and juice were essential. To keep your pack weight to a minimum, be sure you are not taking canned goods, two items when one or the other might do the job of both, and any items that you determine are not necessary to your safety and comfort.

I carry a signal mirror and whistle for emergencies. Every member in a hiking party, not just the children, should carry a whistle and know how and when to use it. Teach your children never to blow on the whistle unless they are in trouble. Also teach them that a signal of three sharp and distinct blows on the whistle indicates someone is in trouble, and it will alert anyone within hearing distance.

You never know when a real need or emergency will arise, so it is best always to be prepared. Know the location of the nearest emergency room. Involve your children in every plan that you make. They are never too young to hear how to take care of themselves. I let someone responsible know where I am going, and I also take someone responsible, such as another adult, along "just in case." You should also learn basic first aid and cardiopulmonary resuscitation (CPR). It is a helpless feeling to be in an emergency and have no idea how to proceed or what to do. The Red Cross is a good place to look for first-aid instruction. No matter what, remember safety first!

Set the pace of the hike to the slowest and weakest member of your hiking team. This is not to embarrass that member of the group, but rather to ensure that the pace is appropriate and nobody gets pushed beyond his limits. Remember, though, that diplomacy is crucial. Fellow playmates will be quick to abuse and tease a "weakling." Whatever reason you give for slowing the pace, pick a positive one.

Children have very sensitive skin, so be prepared with good sunblock. A hat and sunglasses will provide added protection from the sun and heat. Protection from insects is nearly as important as that from the sun. Insect repellent is such a noxious substance, however, that I recommend wearing long sleeves and long pants whenever possible. If using insect repellent becomes necessary, apply it sparingly and keep it away from the eyes and mouth. Insect repellent in the eyes is painful and can become a medical emergency.

Children want and need friends with them, so bring a close family playmate along for your children. Having another friend along makes things more fun for them and usually makes the hike easier for you because it takes you out of the spotlight.

Choosing a destination is perhaps the hardest task of all. Everyone has a favorite memory, most spectacular view, or most unbelievable campsite. What is incredible to one person, however, may not be worth the effort to another. This is especially true with children. Parents quickly learn that fantastic views are not enough to stimulate children into oohs and aahs. Children seem to prefer lakes to splash in, streams to wade through, meadows to romp around, trees to climb up, hills to roll down, easy rocks to scramble on, mud for pies, and someone to play with.

Keeping seasons in mind, I have found that I am able to plan a fairly exciting outing for my daughter and me. Nikki loves colors, smelling wild-flowers, watching insects, skipping rocks on a smooth lake surface, discovering cloud shapes, and rolling down hills with reckless abandon. A trail covered with fall leaves to kick and romp through is an additional enticement. Find out what interests your child and then go for it. Plan your trip around his or her sensory pleasures.

Be prepared to get down and dirty with your children; experiencing the outdoors with them means participating, not watching. Perhaps one of my most vivid memories when I was teaching outdoor education is of a young boy who found it distasteful to get dirty. We were gathered around a camp-fire enjoying gooey s'mores (chocolate bars, toasted marshmallows, and graham crackers all mashed together into a wonderfully messy and delicious sandwich). I happened to glance away from the campfire and noticed a neatly dressed boy standing by himself. Wondering what was wrong, because everyone else was laughing so hard, I encouraged him to join us around the fire. "Naw," he replied, "can't hang with that stuff—too messy, you know." Too bad! Because of his attitude and upbringing (I'd never seen a shinier car than the one that picked him up the next morning), he was unable to fully enjoy the evening with his friends.

This is not to say that you have to get filthy to appreciate being out-doors. A little dirt, however, should not hold you back. When I worked at a summer camp as the trip director and nature instructor, one of the favorite classes was Swamp Mucking. Wading waist-deep through a prepared route into the swamp to view wildlife at eye level brought squeals of delight, even from refined sixteen-year-olds. Interestingly, I had several letters from parents who had heard about the class through their children's letters and wanted to join in. So go for it with your children; you'll never find a better excuse to let your hair down and have fun!

The distance of any trip can be difficult to gauge. How far or how fast can become a guessing game that is contingent upon the mood of the hikers, the weather, and the terrain's difficulty and interest. You really can't do much about the mood of the hikers, short of maintaining your own excellent sense of humor. You also can't do much about the weather—

The outdoors is one giant, adventurous playground for children, full of fun and surprises around every corner.

EXCEPT be prepared for anything with the appropriate clothing and gear. You can, however, plan and control the difficulty of terrain as well as its visual interest.

Plan easy hikes, especially for those group members who may have their doubts about the trip. I recommend no more than five-hundred feet elevation gain and loss and a hike of less than five miles under most circumstances. To virtually guarantee that everyone will have a wonderful time, the hike itself, and not just the destination, must be memorable. Huffing, puffing, and wheezing are memorable, but it's not the kind of memory most children are eager to acquire. Take frequent rest breaks, eat plenty of snacks, splash through a stream or two, play entertaining games, and do whatever comes to mind to have fun.

Pay close attention to your family, because their eyes and voice tone are full of valuable information. Are they looking around eagerly or are they looking at their feet? Are they feeling sore or tired? Is getting to the destination becoming more of a burden than a goal? It is acceptable to turn around at any time—especially if the hike is just as important as the destination. How you turn around, though, will determine whether this hike will be a success. Never make your children feel guilty or try to motivate an exhausted member of your group by cajoling or needling. Make the decision to turn around your idea. You can say that you feel tired, or you can use any other reason that comes to mind and doesn't sound condescending or ridiculous.

If the reasons are right, no one will regret the decision. The mountain or lake will always be there for another try. Your family and children may not be persuaded to go again if the last outing was miserable; they do not want to risk a repeat. Not surprisingly, most of the horror stories that I have heard from parents, children, and other adults usually revolve around someone dragging them over peaks, through deep valleys, through pouring rain, and so on. The essential idea in sharing the outdoors with children is to have fun and expose them to a wonderful world full of discoveries.

Humor and patience are a must. Without them your efforts to share the outdoors will be seriously hampered. Laughter, fun and games, silly pranks, and unexpected events are part of being outdoors with children. Go with the flow and enjoy every moment. If you can learn to laugh off a child who is inadvertently covered with mud and expecting a ride home in the family car, then you are ready to proceed as an outdoor leader. Good luck!

TIPS IN A NUTSHELL

1. Plan a destination that is attractive and fun for all. Keep the hike less than five miles long and the elevation gain and loss to a minimum; five hundred feet is about right. Scenery and interesting things to do and see will spice up any hike.

2. Favorite and nutritional snacks in addition to a tasty lunch are a must. Fruit, Gorp (short for granola, oatmeal, raisins, peanuts), cheese sticks, individual-serving sizes of fruit juice, crackers, and other family favorites can be packed as snacks. Use care when packing any item that is easily crushed or melted. Grapes and candy bars, for example, that have spread all over the inside of a pack aren't very appetizing.

3. Carry the bare minimum in your packs.

4. Everyone should carry some sort of signaling device.

5. Be prepared to get down and dirty with your children. Experience the outdoors with them; don't just watch them.

6. Always have an emergency plan.

7. Adequate sun and insect protection is very important.

8. Bring a family playmate along.

CHAPTER 2

Equipment Needs

BEFORE STARTING ANY ADVENTURE, your family will need to be properly equipped. This has the potential of being more difficult to accomplish than it sounds, because there are many alternatives and choices. Following some basic considerations and guidelines, however, will make the task easier.

Begin by researching equipment available. Talk to friends about what they like and where they shop. Check out magazines that evaluate gear, such as *Backpacker* or *Outside*. Head to your local outdoor store and talk to salespeople about your needs.

Once you have collected and evaluated enough product information, the choices will narrow, and you will be able to make educated and valuable purchasing or borrowing decisions. Many outdoor stores rent sleeping bags, tents, backpacks, stoves, and even child carriers. Some also rent boots; I would discourage this, however, because footwear is a particularly personal item. A rented boot creates the opportunity for hiking misery and a ruined trip.

GENERAL OUTDOOR GEAR

TENT

Picking the best tent for your needs can be a difficult task. If you go camping only with your children, then the decision becomes easier. However, if you, or you and your spouse, like to camp without the kids on occasion, then you must decide to buy either two tents or one tent that is sometimes too small or too large. I solved this dilemma by buying a relatively roomy two-person tent that we used under slightly cramped conditions until Nikki reached age four. I then added a large nylon tarp, which doesn't add much weight to my backpack. The tarp provides an "extra room" under which I am protected while my wife and daughter sleep in the tent. The tarp also provides an extra benefit—something to sit and cook under in bad weather.

When purchasing a tent, buy quality. Blown stitches, waterproof coatings that leak like a sieve, broken cheap fiberglass poles, and torn fabric are all candidates for the Nightmare Weekend Hall of Fame. Be sure that the tent is roomy enough so you don't feel imprisoned, but not so roomy that you need porters to carry it. My tent and tarp have a combined weight of nine pounds.

The tent should have a generous rainfly, which will provide adequate protection against the worst storm and still allow for ventilation and evaporation of condensation. The fabric of the tent body and rainfly should be taut when erected; there should be no obvious sags or baggy material to flap and tear in the wind. The rainfly also should not touch the tent body because this can lead to leaks and condensation problems.

Even the best tents are not indestructible if you don't care for them properly. Never store a tent for long periods in a damp condition. The tent will mildew and be ruined. Don't walk in the tent with boots because this, combined with abrasive sand or dirt, can wear a hole in the tent floor. Periodically clean dirt and grime off the tent with a sponge, warm water, and a mild soap. Never light a stove or lantern in a tent. You not only run the risk of melting fabric and destroying the tent, but it can lead to asphyxiation because of a lack of air exchange. Don't forget to seamseal the tent—ask the salesperson to show you how.

SLEEPING BAG AND PAD

When choosing a sleeping bag, synthetic or down fill becomes a crucial question. Down is lighter in terms of the weight-to-warmth ratio. Down is also more compact. Only synthetic fills such as PolarGuard, Hollofil, and Quallofil, however, will maintain loft and warmth when they are wet. Down turns into a heavy, soggy, cold mess. I always recommend synthetic-filled bags for children. I use a down sleeping bag because of its size and weight, but I am very careful to keep it protected from the elements—I even store it in a waterproof stuff sack.

Mummy-shaped bags do a better job of keeping the body warm than do other shapes, but some people find them too constricting. Don't be afraid to ask the salesperson to lay out the bags you are considering so you can climb into them. If you are buying bags to zip together, be sure the zippers are compatible and you purchase right- and left-zipper bags. The other bag shapes are semirectangular and rectangular. Most bags are constructed of nylon or nylon blends inside and out. Sleeping bags with cotton insides, quilted rectangular shapes, and entertaining figures printed on them are not recommended for backpacking or serious outdoor use.

BACKPACK

There are hundreds of styles of backpacks on the market, and everyone has his favorite for an equal number of excellent reasons. Just because your best friend likes his, however, doesn't mean you will feel comfortable in the same model. Try on any backpack that you are considering, and have the salesperson put thirty to forty pounds in it so you can compare and walk around.

Internal-frame backpacks offer close fit, low center of gravity, flexibility, and a relative freedom of movement to the user. They do not, however, carry unwieldy loads easily, and they can become unstable and uncomfortable if you must lash large amounts of gear to the outside of the pack. There's a prevalent myth that internal-frame packs are significantly hotter to wear than external frames. This is not so.

External-frame backpacks are rigid, restrict movement, and have a higher center of gravity. Unlike an internal frame, however, the rigid frame can carry ridiculously awkward loads quite comfortably and offers numerous lash points for attaching items—useful for the parent who has to carry most everything while the other parent carries the child.

Buying a backpack for a child is a little less complex. I would recommend that children less than eight years old carry nothing more than a day pack. If you can find one with a waist strap, which helps prevent the pack from bouncing around on your child's back, he will find it much more comfortable to carry.

As your child gets older and expresses an interest in carrying more (usually between the ages of eight and ten), it is time to consider buying a child-size frame pack. Both Kelty and Camptrails make aluminum-frame packs for children that have a certain amount of adjustability built in to allow the pack to grow with the child. The pack, however, must fit well; a pack that bounces and sways on your child's back is extremely uncomfortable and top-heavy. It sets the scenario for a miserable child and a ruined experience.

The shoulder straps and bar to which they are attached should rest, when the pack is loaded, between the top of the shoulders and the base of the skull. The waist belt should comfortably cup the hips; not so high that it compresses the stomach nor so low that it sits on the buttocks.

STOVE

There was once a time when campfires were the way to cook and you used a stove for convenience or backup. Now, however, wood in many camping sites is being overused and is sometimes nonexistent. As more people enjoy our wilderness, using stoves becomes a much more ecologically responsible decision. There are no scarring fire rings, no charred wood is scattered around, and no wood is removed from the environment.

There are quite a number of backpacking stoves on the market. You are faced with one major choice: white gas or butane/propane. White-gas stoves typically burn hotter, boil water more quickly, and can be pressurized with an external pump. On the down side, you have to prime white-gas stoves, the pumping can be a hassle, and they require more frequent cleaning and maintenance. Butane stoves are more convenient to use. You just turn on the gas and light them. Each cartridge is self-pressurized, however, so cold temperatures or a near-empty cartridge will negatively affect the efficiency and heat output of the stove.

Never light a stove in a tent, and never allow children to operate it while unsupervised. Ask the salesperson to show you how to safely light and maintain your stove before you leave the store with your purchase.

KITCHEN

Assembling a kit for your camp kitchen is actually quite easy. With a few careful purchases and some items from your home kitchen, you will be able to put together a very serviceable kit. First, you will need to buy a good set of nesting pots. I prefer to use stainless steel pots even though they are heavier than aluminum, because aluminum has been reported to harm the body over time and, more practically, they scratch, flake, and dent more easily. Add a good pot grip (a mechanical handle that securely grabs the lip of each pot), a GI-issue folding can opener, and a Teflon fry pan with a folding handle and lid. I also carry an Opinal folding knife that I use only for cooking. The blade stays extremely sharp, locks in place for security, and is inexpensive and light.

For carrying spices I recommend buying a number of small one-ounce nalgene bottles with screw-on lids. Also, pick up a few one-ounce bottles with flip-top nozzles for liquids and oils. More on what to put in these in chapter 3.

From your home kitchen, take an old wooden spoon, a nylon spatula, and several small metal spoons. A tiny whisk is handy for mixing dried milk, pancake mix, hot cocoa, and so on—lumpy drinks and food are not the way to win over your critics.

Pack the pots in one stuff sack, the utensils in a second smaller sack, and the spices in a very small see-through ditty bag. The stuff sack for the pots will help prevent the inside of your pack and other items from becoming as black as the pots.

If you are planning to cook over a fire, add a pair of cotton or light leather gloves to your kit. They will help prevent burns and keep your hands cleaner.

A knife, fork, and spoon are deemed essential. To lighten the load, consider that a spoon can do almost everything a fork can do, but not vice versa. I leave the fork at home. If each person is carrying a pocket knife, then there is no need to pack knives just for eating purposes.

When deciding to pack eating implements, such as a plate, bowl, and cup, think light. The kit for each member of our family consists of a wide-bottomed cup and a plastic plate with deep sides that can double as a bowl. Children spill things very easily, so whatever you choose, be sure that it is stable when full of food or drink. Also, the less a child has to hold or worry about, the less likely he or she will spill.

As an added tip, take one or two of the cups you plan on bringing and etch or mark measurements on the inside. I have marked ounces up the side of mine so that I can accurately measure ingredients in the field. Some camp cups sold at outdoor stores already have the markings on them.

TEN ESSENTIALS

The "Ten Essentials" was a name coined to describe those particular items that are necessary to a person's survival should an emergency arise. The original ten items expanded on many lists to include some of the bare essentials necessary to ensure basic comfort and not just survival (for example, the addition of toilet paper).

The original Ten Essentials are: topographic map, compass, flashlight with extra bulb and batteries, extra food, extra clothing (including rain gear), sunglasses and sunscreen, pocket knife, waterproof matches, firestarter or candle, and first-aid kit.

Other pieces of equipment that are strongly recommended and begin to expand the list are: water bottle, ground insulator (such as an Ensolite pad), emergency blanket, tub shelter or rain fly, and signaling devices (such as signal flares, mirror, or whistle).

Your list of essentials may grow as your family needs dictate. You should also take into account the activity choice to help you determine what is essential and what isn't. Different equipment items become necessary when switching from a backpacking trip to a canoe, bicycle, or cross-country ski outing.

CARRYING YOUR CHILD

Introducing your child to the outdoors before he or she can realistically walk any distance is a great way to get them excited about wilderness. It does, however, require that you act as mule and papoose carrier. The thought of adding extra and very shifty weight to the load already expected sends shudders down the spines of many would-be camping parents. A word of comfort to soothe the shudders: The gentle rocking rhythm of a walking parent is often enough to put the squirmiest child to rest.

Although a good child carrier is not cheap, it is worth its price for the carrying comfort, support, and versatility provided to both parent and child. There are two types of carrier: the soft snuggle sack that hangs in front of the parent for those children who are too young to sit up, and the frame-support carriers for older children who weigh up to thirty-five pounds.

The snuggle sack is probably best typified by the Snugli carrier. Its crisscross carrying design is quite comfortable. The baby is supported by an adjustable seat and rests inside a soft cotton-lined pouch. You wear the carrier slung in front for very young babies or over your back for larger infants. The main limitation is that its soft design affords no real support for the parent during extended carries. I found this system ideal for my newborn, for example, but quickly moved into something with more support once Nikki could sit up.

Larger frame-style child carriers come in a variety of designs and comfort levels. The best way to decide what will work best for you and your child is to try the carriers, with the child on board, and compare the fit and feel. Your choices will vary from a simple plastic frame with minimal shoulder straps and a basic seat sling to intricate aluminum welded frames with sturdy and well padded suspensions similar to the most advanced expedition pack.

Some carriers will face the child forward and others backward. I have found that in backward-facing carriers the child sometimes feels more like baggage and is unable to see where he or she is going. This inevitably results in squirming and shifting while the child attempts to turn around—leaving you to carry a rather unwieldy load that keeps jerking you off your center of gravity. Nikki learned to shift her weight at calculated moments, getting Dad to stumble and give her thrill-a-minute giggles—and Dad an extra rush of adrenaline!

Child carriers that have the child facing forward seem to put the child closer to your center of gravity, which translates into a more natural gait and stride for you. Because the child can easily see where he is going, he is more comfortable and more at ease. There is a downside to front-facing children, however—wandering little hands that love to pull hair, stick fingers in your mouth, and inadvertently poke eyes.

Before you decide on a particular model, make sure that the system you choose is sturdily built and comes equipped with a safety belt with which to strap in your child. An untimely trip or fall could catapult an unbelted child into space, resulting in a nasty injury. Also choose a carrier that features a built-in fold-out stand that will support the carrier upright on the ground. You will find this characteristic wonderful for quick rest stops. Don't ever leave your child unattended in a carrier!

CHILDREN'S CLOTHING

Clothing needs will depend on several basic elements, such as the age of your children, your definition of dirty, and how much you are willing to carry. Babies and toddlers will need more clothing because they are more likely to soil a garment inside and out. Stretch one-piece suits are ideal for this age group because they not only protect the body from the elements, but help protect against insects as well. The older the child is, the less changes he or she is likely to require—all depending, of course, on your taste in cleanliness.

As a planning guide for teens, I suggest one change of underwear for each day, one extra shirt, one extra pair of pants, a bathing suit (boys' swim trunks can double as shorts or vice versa), and one pair of socks (including liner and outer) for each day. For ages six to twelve, plan on a fresh shirt for each day and add an extra pair of pants. With children under six, I plan on one complete outfit for each day, plus several extra clean and warm outfits for sleeping and emergency ("How did you get that so dirty?") use. The above suggestions are maximum suggestions—if you can do with less, you will be the happier for it.

Diapers are a necessary pain in the wilderness. Some parents stand by cloth diapers and wash them when camping. I hate washing dirty diapers in a warm pot of sudsy water, and if the weather is wet they will not dry. Instead, I opt for disposable diapers. You do have a choice between those that have their own plastic overpant and those with a reusable overpant. Let your environmental ethic be the guide.

Do not attempt to bury the diaper, because the adverse environmental impact of this practice is not only ugly, it is permanent. It is possible to burn the diaper's fiber filling (removing the plastic pant if attached) if your fire is hot enough. Keep in mind that the resulting odor is unpleasant and that the fire must be very hot and maintained until the diaper is burned completely. You must pack out any of the remains that do not burn. My personal preference is to pack out the diaper and bury the human waste. Just as you would dispose of your own solid waste, bury the contents of the diaper four to six inches below the soil level. Double-bag the soiled diaper in a garbage sack and then put it in a large nylon stuff sack, which you can attach to the outside of your pack. The nylon stuff sack will protect the contents from ripping open and is easily hung when in bear country.

Washing clothes during your trip will greatly reduce the number of extra outfits that you need to carry for your child; there are, however, some inherent drawbacks. You will be dependent on warm and sunny weather to dry the clothes—if it is wet and the clothes do not dry, what then? I also do not find being tied to a wash basin and clothesline my idea of a wilderness escape. Spend too much time performing chores and you end up with nothing more than a wilderness version of your normal housekeeping duties, which doesn't leave much time to enjoy the wilds and wonders you are trying to share.

The material and color of the clothing is very important. Avoid the color blue because it seems to more readily attract mosquitoes and gnats than do other colors. For younger children who are inclined to wander, select bright colors that stand out and are easily spotted. Look for synthetic materials, too. Synthetics are lighter, provide excellent insulation, and dry faster than their natural counterparts. Select materials made of pile, bunting, polypropylene, Capilene, Thermax, Synchilla, and so on.

Natural fibers work well, too, but you must understand their limitations. Cotton is great as a nonirritating fiber next to the skin and for keeping the body cool. It absorbs moisture extremely well, however, so it has no insulating value and takes forever to dry. Its usage should be limited to warm weather. Wool is a superb insulator, even when wet, but it can irritate the skin, leaving children and parents more frustrated than warm. Continual scratching is not indicative of having a good time. Wool is probably best limited to socks and outerwear such as pants and sweaters.

When planning what your children will wear, think in terms of a three-level layering. The first layer will be the wicking layer or underwear. This is followed by one or two insulating layers depending on need: either a sweater or a jacket or both. The final layer is the outer shell to offer protection from wind and moisture. Effectively planned, a layering system will allow you to remove or add clothing as your child's body temperature and environmental conditions dictate.

The inner layer is best made out of polypropylene, Thermax, or Capilene. A number of outdoor companies now make underwear for children. The insulative layer should consist of items such as a wool sweater, a wool or synthetic vest, and/or a pile, Synchilla, or bunting jacket. For the outer layer, I recommend a waterproof nylon jacket and pants. The rain-suit type of outerwear affords far more protection than a mere poncho and is a lot easier to romp and play in. Several companies now make

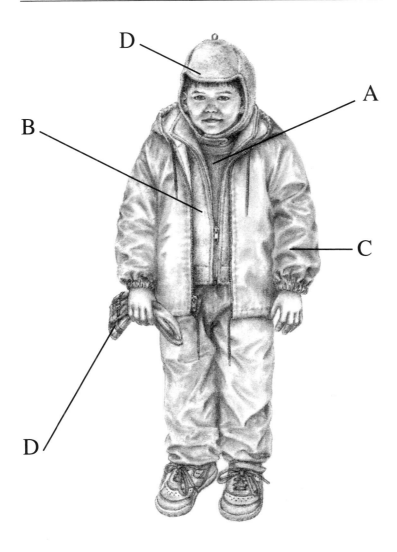

*Properly layered clothing will help keep children comfortable at all times.
A—Layer of thin insulation (underwear). B—Second layer of insulation
(sweater, jacket). C—Protective third layer (rainproof and windproof).
D—Hat and mittens.*

rain suits with reflective tape for easy spotting by flashlight—I like this feature.

As you are shopping for these various items, shock and horror may set in when you discover that the miniaturized versions of the adult gear cost just as much. Weigh this financial fact with the prospect that the little one will probably soon outgrow the outfit and the economic implications of camping with children seem daunting. Not to worry. Not every item needs to come from a specialty outdoor store. Used children's clothing is a growing business, so look in flea markets, thrift shops, and other sources. Some of the latter are friends and other families with whom you can get acquainted through hiking clubs and camping groups.

Another way to extend your dollar is to buy clothing with growth in mind. When buying pants, for example, purchase a pair with an adjustable or elastic waistband that will expand as your child grows. Most younger children tend to grow more in length than in width, so do not be afraid to buy clothing a little long: you can always roll up the excess at the ankles or arms. Some manufacturers make clothes with growth adjustments built in.

While some companies make hiking boots for children, most children seem to prefer tennis shoes. I must admit, however, that Nikki likes hiking boots; putting on her boots makes her feel like an accomplished explorer and ready for anything. I have the feeling that as she gets older, perhaps even this summer, she will toss aside the explorer image and opt for light-footed freedom.

Boots, however, are the only appropriate choice when severe weather or rugged or snowy terrain are expected. If you buy boots for your child, make sure they are very comfortable. Most children's hiking boots are lightweight with combination nylon/leather uppers and fairly flexible lug soles. Look for soles that provide a fair amount of friction so that, when running or jumping, children will not slip or slide. Also be sure to fit the boots with your child wearing the socks that he or she will use hiking. (If thicker wool socks will be worn on the hike, fitting the boots with cotton tube socks virtually guarantees a boot that jams the toes and cramps the feet.) The fit should be snug in the heel, roomy in the toes, and nonbinding. Do not buy a boot with the intention of having your child wear extra socks until he or she grows into them. Doing so is an open invitation to blisters and other discomforts.

TIPS IN A NUTSHELL

1. Thoroughly research available products using catalogs, magazines such as *Backpacker* and *Outside*, friends' opinions, and a specialty-store salesperson's advice.

2. Rent when and where you can. Many specialty stores will rent tents, backpacks, sleeping bags, stoves, and child carriers. Avoid renting boots.

3. Buy quality whenever the budget will allow.

4. Borrow as much old cooking gear from your home kitchen as possible. Leave anything extra at home to save weight. Be sure that bowls for children are sturdy and won't tip easily.

5. Always pack and carry the Ten Essentials.

6. Be sure that your child carrier has free-standing capability, is comfortable for both you and the child, has a seat belt, and is sturdily built.

7. Never bury diapers outdoors—always carry out what you carry in.

8. Select brightly colored clothing to keep your children visible (stay away from the color blue). Choose clothes made from synthetics because these materials will dry out more readily than natural fibers.

9. Dress your child in layers: underwear; then insulative layers depending on need; then rain wear for wind and moisture protection.

10. Most younger children prefer tennis shoes to hiking boots. Boots are appropriate if weather or difficult hiking conditions dictate more foot protection (for example, when hiking in snow, loose rocks, and wet or muddy terrain). Children should be wearing the socks they will be hiking in when boots are fitted.

CHAPTER 3

Planning the Trip

P LANNING IS AN IMPORTANT phase for children to be involved in if they are to become part of the adventure. In the long run, it is important for you to spend the extra minutes it will take to teach children how to repackage food, how to lay out gear so they can see what they are packing, how to load a pack, and how to check equipment for safety and function. Only when the parent ends up assuming all the tasks does the prospect of a family camping trip become tedious for the parent and uninteresting for the children.

CHOOSING THE DESTINATION

Taking your family on an extended camping trip for the first time can be a somewhat uncertain proposition, even if you have successfully completed every preparatory step from the backyard camp to state park day-hikes to a campground overnight. While flexibility and a positive attitude are important, proper planning and choosing an appropriate destination should reign supreme; it will go far in minimizing potential pitfalls.

Spend as much time as you can with the family poring over all the information available about the particular areas you would like to visit. Magazines, books, park flyers, travelogues, and state or provincial promotional brochures are all excellent resources for initial exploration. Appendix III has a list of magazines that will be helpful in this endeavor. For detailed guidebooks about particular destinations, check the book department of your local specialty outdoor store.

What you and your family can do to make this process most productive is ask yourselves a number of questions. What are your activity interests—fishing, hiking, scrambling, climbing, swimming? How important is seeing wildlife—deer, bear, squirrels, skunks, raccoons? Will studying the stars or viewing vast fields of wildflowers be important? What is the maximum easy hiking distance your family can handle? How near to the parking area or car do you wish to be in case of emergencies? What kind of temperature and weather does your family prefer—foggy, sunny, rainy, snowy, variety? What kind of topographic relief are you looking for in the terrain—rolling, flat, mountainous, swampy? Is your family interested in historical events or the historical significance of particular areas—Yukon Gold Rush, Donner Party, Cumberland Gap? Once you have determined answers to these and any other questions you deem important to your family, then the planning can begin in earnest.

One other question that should not be overlooked is this: How long and how difficult is the drive getting to and from the chosen site? This may not seem like a major consideration, but try sitting in a car for more than four hours with children craving and counting on activity and you have a recipe for frustration, aggravation, and a potential "I hate this, why didn't we just stay home," response. Not an ideal way to begin a family outing.

Once your family has decided on a potential area by reading and researching, try talking to people who have been there. Find out from them what the area is really like. Firsthand experience is invaluable for obtaining specific information such as the location of hidden hot springs, the best place to fish, the ideal campsite, seasonal insect populations, bear or other animal precautions, difficulty of terrain, and so on.

Finally, after all the information has been taken in and a potential destination determined, take one final look at the information and compare it honestly against your family's physical and emotional abilities. Is the destination a good choice for maximum fun and safety? If the answer remains yes, your destination is selected and equipment planning begins. If the answer is no or maybe, then pick something a little less ambitious for this first trip. You can always progress to your first choice when your family has more outdoor experience.

Once the destination has been chosen, you need to obtain detailed information. This involves purchasing United States Geological Survey (USGS)

Children feel more a part of the adventure when allowed to carry their own packs.

topographic maps for the area, National Forest Service maps, trail guide-books, and other privately produced maps of the area if available. You cannot have too much information in this planning stage. Of course, you will probably only pack along the topographic maps and, maybe, the guidebook. In appendix V there is a listing of addresses and sources for this type of information.

Plot your route carefully on the maps. Many of the USGS topo maps were last surveyed in the early to late 1950s; revisions and updates (often visually checked by aerial survey) are slow in coming. Transcribing detailed information regarding trails, roads, and other man-made landmarks from forest service and private maps and guidebooks to the topos is most helpful. If you are lucky, the private maps will be reproductions of the USGS maps with all the necessary trail and hiking data updated and transcribed for you.

Wilderness with Children

FIELD CHECK ALL EQUIPMENT

Our family finds it helpful to put all equipment in plain view on the living room floor. While this tends to make the room look like it has been the victim of a small nuclear explosion, it does serve to keep all items in plain view and makes it easy to determine if we have everything necessary for the trip. As Nikki, my wife, or I call out the items on our checklist, one of us puts that item to one side to be checked and packed.

All equipment gets checked. We examine pots for cleanliness; stoves for fuel and function (a stove that will not light is more easily repaired at home than the field); flashlights for power; knives for sharpness; tent for tears and dirt; sleeping bags for loft, cleanliness, and tears; sleeping pads for air leaks; packs for tears and frame cracks; and the first-aid kit for contents. The first-aid kit requires very careful checking to ensure that all medications have not expired, that all materials are clean and stocked, and that any items last used have been either replaced or sterilized.

Finally, with all our planned items (except food) spread on the floor, we go through the list to determine if we are leaving anything out or if we are packing too much. Always operate under the KISS principle—Keep It Simple, Stupid. Pack and carry as little as is necessary to be comfortable and safe. If in doubt, leave it behind. If two items will do a similar job, choose the one that suits the purpose best and leave the other home.

MENU PLANNING

When putting together a menu for your trip, don't overlook the importance of taste, nutrition, and energy content. Adults and children need high-energy carbohydrate foods when adventuring outdoors. This is not to say that your family's diet should become one of sugar and fat during a wilderness excursion. Planning meals and snacks that include pasta, milk, cheese, rice, seeds, nuts, dried fruit, and vegetables will adequately meet nutritional needs for you and your children. Weight, ease of packaging and handling, and variety are also necessary considerations.

Water is a critical addition to menu planning. It is vital that each person

Nutritious and tasty snacks are an important part of any outing.

in your family drink two to three quarts of water each day. Proper hydration will help prevent hypothermia, heat stroke, heat cramps, frostbite, and altitude sickness. Just as important is the need to maintain the body's balance of water and salt. The normal diet typically includes an adequate provision of salt in your meals without the need to add more. If the trip is extremely difficult, or the weather unusually hot, then an electrolyte additive to the water is appropriate. But be careful not to overdo the salt, because too much salt is more harmful than too little.

Weight may be reduced by combining dried, dehydrated, and freeze-

Wilderness with Children

dried foods along with any fresh selections in your menu. Further lighten your load by repacking everything into Ziploc plastic bags. Choose sturdy freezer-quality bags, not flimsy sandwich ones. Stay away from canned goods.

I have found that it is more convenient and more efficient to prepackage meals in a large freezer-variety Ziploc bag. If it is possible, I premeasure and premix all the dry ingredients together in the same bag. Don't forget to label the bag with its contents and, unless you have an incredible memory, drop in brief written instructions with each meal.

Spoilage is a problem when camping without the benefit of a cooler. Stay away from real butter, cooked meats, eggs, and noncanned bacon. Real cheese such as cheddar and Muenster is fine outdoors and does not spoil, but processed cheeses and spreads do spoil and should be avoided. The softer the cheese, the higher the oil content, the more the cheese will turn gooey. I prefer to carry hard cheeses such as Jarlsberg or Gouda.

The ultimate rule is to plan your meals and snacks so that they will be easy and fun to prepare, visually appealing, and tasty. The following list has been compiled to aid you in your menu planning. Don't forget to solicit your children's input as well.

BREAKFAST SUGGESTIONS

Drinks: cocoa, orange juice crystals or Tang, tea, coffee, low-fat dried milk

Cereal: oatmeal, Cream of Wheat, Malto Meal, Cream of Rice, granola, 7-grain

Main dishes: pancake mix (Bisquick works well), western omelet (freeze dried), mixed fruit (freeze dried)

Dried fruit: apricots, prunes, raisins, apples, pineapples, plums, cherries, pears, peaches

TRAIL LUNCH SUGGESTIONS:

Meat: bacon bits or bar, jerky (beef or turkey), salami, pemmican, beef stick

Cheese: any nonpasteurized, nonprocessed cheese that does not require refrigeration

Nuts: peanuts, pecans, cashews, pine nuts, walnuts, hazelnuts, almonds

Seeds: pumpkin, sunflower, soya, sesame

Fresh vegetables: carrots, radishes, cauliflower, jicama, celery, turnips, broccoli

Fresh fruits: apples, oranges, tangerines

Dried or freeze-dried fruits: dates, apples, pineapples, bananas, peaches, prunes, apricots, raisins

Breads/crackers/pastries: Lebanese flat bread, sourdough, rye, pilot biscuits, Ritz, Waverly, Triscuits, Rye-Crisps, Japanese rice crackers, Cheese Nips, melba toast, trail biscuits, Pop-Tarts, Danishes

Sweets: licorice, Tootsie Rolls, lemon drops, candy orange slices, tropical chocolate, malted-milk tablets, Life Savers, fruit bars, sesame seed bars, pudding (various flavors in small aluminum cans—pack out the cans), cookies

Drinks: Kool-Aid, Wylers, juice crystals, Tang, hot cocoa (nothing better for a cold day), individual serving size boxes of juice

DINNER SUGGESTIONS

Drinks: Wylers, Kool-Aid, tea, coffee, hot cocoa, Tang

Soups: Lipton and Knorr instants, Top Ramen, freeze dried from outdoor-specialty store

Freeze-dried dinners: Richmoor, Natural High, Backpacker Pantry, AlpineAire, Weepak, and Mountain House. (If you have never tried freeze-dried dinners before, buy several, take them home, and prepare them. I must admit a personal preference to Backpacker Pantry desserts and side dishes and AlpineAire and Natural High main courses, but everyone's tastes are different.)

Meal staples and mixes: textured vegetable protein made of soy bean and good added to soups or casserole; Uncle Ben's Quick Brown Rice; Bisquick; pastas; lentils, pinto and lima beans; corn-bread mixes; instant potatoes; Miso, tomato base, chicken base, beef base, instant gravy or sauce packets; freeze-dried chicken, beef, and fish; freeze-dried vegetables

SPICES AND ADDITIVES

cinnamon sugar

Squeeze Parkay, Country Crock, or other margarine

Crisco in small container (Better than oils and butter for cooking and frying, and it doesn't burn or break down as easily on a hot flame. After each use, pour back into container and reuse.)

honey (Healthier than white sugar for sweetening. Package in a squeeze tube or eight-ounce nalgene bottle.)

peanut butter and honey mix (Premix two parts peanut butter to one part honey and package in squeeze tube.)

brown sugar (alternative to honey and not as messy)

dry milk (Make into a paste before adding all the water required to help prevent lumping.)

cinnamon, nutmeg, curry, oregano, chili powder, garlic, black pepper, salt, dry mustard (Package each in one-ounce nalgene bottles and label.)

soy sauce—the backpacker's ketchup

Worchestershire sauce and Tabasco sauce (Package in flip-top bottles for spicing up otherwise somewhat bland freeze-dried meals.)

bouillon cubes or powder

FAVORITE MEAL SUGGESTIONS

Breakfast: pancakes and wild-berry syrup, hot cocoa or orange juice crystals, dried fruit

Lunch: Gorp, peanut butter and honey mix on Ritz crackers or Party Rye bread, beef jerky, Wylers Lemonade Mix or water, candy bar.

Dinner: freeze-dried spaghetti mix, Knorr instant vegetable soup, instant chocolate pudding (using instant milk), Tang, Wylers, or water.

REPACKAGING FOOD

If you don't own stock interest in the Ziploc Company, consider buying some. Ziploc self-sealing plastic bags are a camper's best friend. Much of your food, with the exception of fresh produce, should get repackaged into them. Fresh produce is best carried in a breathable mesh bag near the top or to the outside of a pack because produce tends to spoil in plastic unless refrigerated.

Bulk and frequently used foods will get packaged in either double freezer Ziploc bags or one-quart nalgene bottles with wide mouths. For beverages, sugar, milk, and coffee, I prefer wide-mouth nalgene bottles. They are easier to frequently open and close, are more easily handled by little hands, and won't tear or break. Food items such as Bisquick, flour, pasta, dried fruits, and so on will pack and carry nicely in a double-bag Ziploc system. I recommend double bagging to prevent accidental bursting and puncturing in your pack.

Setting up a mini-assembly line with you, your spouse, and older children performing the measuring tasks and label writing is an efficient and fun method to repackage foods and meals. Younger children will enjoy sealing the bags (be sure to squeeze out all the air) and sticking on the labels.

A fun thing to try, if you want a little fresh food on your outing, is to grow sprouts. You can obtain seeds from a health-food store as well as specific instructions on how to grow them. The basic idea is to take some alfalfa seeds, place them in a smaller Ziploc bag, keep the seeds moist, and rinse with fresh water every day. Each child can be put in charge of cultivating his or her own plastic-bag garden for mealtime. They will enjoy watching the seeds sprout while on the trip.

PACKING THE GEAR

Packing isn't as hard as it sounds. With all the gear still out on the living room floor, and the food arranged by meals and days, begin loading the packs. The rough rule of thumb is to keep heavier items close to your center of gravity, your back, and not too high or too low in the pack. For men this is usually higher on the back next to the shoulders. Women will tend to be more comfortable if they pack heavier weights lower and more toward the middle of the pack—just above the small of the back and next to the frame. Work your way out with medium-weight items; finally, the lightest items should be placed in the most distant corners of your pack.

Children should be carefully supervised when loading their packs. Smaller, younger children want to be involved, but they should not carry much more than two or three small and fairly lightweight items. Older children will be able to carry more, but beware of allowing them to become pack mules, restricting their freedom to play and romp—the reason you are heading into the wilderness with them in the first place.

Teenagers should be allowed to carry more, but be careful of egos here. Children can attempt to carry too much to impress their friends and family, and they can exhaust or injure themselves. Other children will begin to feel very self-conscious about not being able to carry what they perceive as their fair share. This is a very vulnerable age and emotions must be handled tenderly. I have found it most effective to play down the importance of carrying larger loads and to emphasize wilderness skills that anyone can acquire. Campfire building, map and weather reading, and food preparation are the more important skills, not who can carry the heaviest load. When I worked as a camp counselor, I found that if a teenager was gung ho to carry a large load, I was the first to begin unloading my pack on them to create the idea that carrying a heavy load is not such a desirable plan.

The younger the children, the more the parents must carry. It is quite conceivable that one parent will end up carrying the bulk of the family gear and food while the other parent carries a child and the rest of the equipment. If one parent is carrying a ridiculously heavy and awkward load, I recommend hiking a short way to a wilderness base camp. Once at the base camp, your family can enjoy a wide and varied wilderness experience on day-hikes and, if necessary, you can still hike to the vehicles to retrieve cached gear or food.

TIPS IN A NUTSHELL

1. Use magazines, guidebooks, park flyers, promotional brochures, and travelogues to help you plan your destination. Involve the entire family in the planning process. Additional and valuable sources of information are USGS topo maps, forest service maps, and privately produced area maps.

2. Determine family needs and interests—fishing, hiking, scrambling, climbing, swimming, wildlife observation, history, and so on.

3. Keep driving distances to and from the destination to a minimum. Four hours is long enough in a car if you expect the children to be eager about the hike.

4. Check all equipment carefully before heading afield. A stove is much

more easily repaired at home than in the wilderness with the entire family waiting hungrily for dinner—vultures make better company when this occurs.

5. Plan the menu based on taste, nutrition, energy, ease of packaging, ease of handling, variety, and spoilage. Be sure children are actively involved in menu planning and that some of their favorite foods are included.

6. Plan on two to three quarts of water per person per day.

7. Combine freeze-dried, dehydrated, dried, and fresh foods to help keep weight to a minimum. Repack all foods from cans, bottles, and boxes in Ziploc bags.

8. Be sure that pack weight is as evenly distributed as possible. Try to avoid one parent becoming pack mule for the clan. Keep children's packs light and prevent teenagers from taking too much.

CHAPTER 4

The Family Camping Trip

O NCE YOU HAVE LEFT your car and begun the voyage to camp, motivational challenges may arise. Children's minds tend to wander, and, if not entertained with variety, the sameness and perceived drudgery of hiking can turn into a continual and very irritating whining. Although playing games and providing entertainment for children is not why most adults head to the wilderness, try to remember that you are striving to create a positive and enticing atmosphere. If heading up a hill chugging like a train and pulling on an imaginary whistle works, go for it.

Singing songs, playing I Spy, fantasizing that you are on a secret exploration, and noting interesting animal signs are all techniques successfully used by parents and camp counselors to maintain interest. Remember that while you may hit on an idea that will work well for twenty minutes or so, nothing works forever or every time. Use variety and capitalize on a child's wonderful imagination.

Children tend to hike in rapid spurts of energy. Watch for this and keep the hiking pace slow and steady, so that they don't wear out tiny legs too soon. As you walk, use generous amounts of encouragement and keep reinforcing how well your children are doing and how far they have come.

Favorite treats are often used as a motivational tool, although I try to play this down with other children and rarely practice it with my own child. This attitude seems to border on buying a behavior and encourages eating as a reward. This is not to belittle the need for tasty or regular food breaks, but with my family they are just that—regular food breaks and not something I use to get junior to walk from point A to B in a pinch.

Try to keep your breaks frequent. On average, plan on a rest break every thirty minutes. Packs come off, snacks come out, water is passed around, and children should be encouraged to sit and rest.

Often, you will find children enjoy being a leader of the group. Put them in the front of the pack and allow them to lead you up the trail and set the pace. I have found that even very tired children will perk up and stride along happily when put in front and in charge. Watch that the child's sudden enthusiasm for being a leader does not translate into a short-lived and maniacal pace.

SETTING UP CAMP

Setting up a campsite can be a wonderful family activity, but if your children are too tired to help productively, they are better off being left to play and rest quietly. Be sure to immediately establish firm play boundaries around camp that they are not to go beyond without a parent. You should be aware of poisonous plants, steep banks by a river, loose rocks near a cliff, dead trees that might topple, and so on. Be sure your children are aware of any dangers that they should avoid. Also, be sure not to set up camp beside, or directly under, any of the aforementioned hazards.

If it has been raining or is somewhat cold, the first task should be to set up the tent and get the family dry and warm. Almost at the same time, you will want to get a fire or stove going for hot drinks. There is nothing like hot chocolate or even hot flavored gelatin to put the sparkle back in a child's eye.

I carry an extra nine-foot-by-nine-foot nylon tarp with grommets at the sides and corners and fifty feet of extra cord. In the event of a wet trip, I set up the tarp near the fire (taking care that sparks and flame won't destroy the tarp) or over the stove for all to sit under while eating, reading, or playing quiet games.

Be sure to establish well-defined kitchen, toilet, waste disposal bag, and sleeping areas. Organization is the key to a successful camp. Food and cooking equipment should be in one clearly designated area while personal

A properly set up camp clearly separates organized kitchen and sleeping areas and minimizes any impact on the surrounding wilderness.

gear and what is needed for washing and cleaning up is in another. Backpacks should be leaning against a tree or rock, sheltered from possible inclement weather and near the tent. Once the camp is set up, you can kick back and enjoy the surroundings to their fullest.

WILDERNESS ETHIC AROUND CAMP
It is very important that you set an example of wilderness ethics for your children to follow. Waste disposal, personal hygiene, cooking, cleaning, and camp setup and break-down all have an impact on the surrounding environment. Your actions will determine whether your visit is a damaging one or goes relatively unnoticed.

When setting up the tent, pick an area that offers durable ground or duff and not a grassy area that is easily matted. Be sure that the tent area has good drainage away from it and will not leave you playing captain to a sinking ship in the midst of a downpour. It is never appropriate to dig drainage ditches around a tent. The ditches leave a permanent scar and rarely work as intended.

Campfires are becoming less acceptable as a means of heat and cooking. Stoves are more environmentally sound. Yet the romance of a crackling fire under a crisp, starlit night is a wonderful experience. Let your conscience be your guide. If you choose to have a fire, there are some guidelines to keep in mind. Never break branches or twigs from a tree, even if they appear to be dead. To do so may cause irreparable damage to the tree. When collecting wood for the fire, choose smaller branches and wood that will burn easily and completely. Go beyond the immediate area of the campsite to collect wood and never, ever burn the last deadfall in the area—if wood seems sparse, use your stove.

When disposing of human waste, the cat-hole method is recommended. This involves digging a hole no deeper than six inches and at least one hundred feet away from the nearest water source. Teach your children to defecate in the hole, but not to bury their toilet paper. Toilet paper must be burned or carried out. Older and responsible children, those who can safely handle matches, should be taught how to burn the paper at the site, making sure all flames are out before leaving the area. I know of one group, camping in Baja, California, that started a major fire because someone did not make sure his burning toilet paper was extinguished before leaving. Be sure that younger children, probably those ten and less, are taught to bring back the used toilet paper to you in a bag for burning under supervision.

If your family is going to base camp in one place for a while, then digging cat holes all around the area each time someone needs to go to the toilet is not a good practice. In this instance you will want to create a latrine or toilet area. Dig a hole approximately one foot deep by one foot across. Ideally, the latrine should be dug in organic matter, and not mineral soil, because bacteria will more rapidly decompose waste in organic matter. Care must be taken when burning toilet paper in organic debris because a fire can easily start. I advise all toilet paper be brought back to a central site, such as the campfire, for burning. Leave a trowel by the hole; a small amount of dirt sprinkled over each deposit of human waste helps minimize flies and encourages decomposition.

Wilderness with Children

Changing diapers in the wilderness is not much different than at home. Be sure to bury the human waste and pack out the rest.

When washing dishes, brushing teeth, and washing the face and hands, do so over a sump hole that is dug twenty-five feet from camp and at least one hundred feet from the nearest water source. The sump hole should drain well and not be any deeper than six inches. The idea behind the sump hole is to allow waste water to drain away and yet catch solid materials, such as food waste, for burning later or packing out.

When filling in a cat hole, latrine, or sump hole, use loose earth, pine needles, leaves, and twigs. Gently pack down the earth and try to match its appearance to that of the surrounding terrain.

Any waste that is not burned should be packed out. Under no circumstances is it acceptable to bury anything in the ground. Watch that younger children do not carelessly drop candy wrappers around camp or on the trail. An excellent way to establish the proper tone is to set up a nylon trash sack immediately upon reaching camp. Then have everyone walk around and pick up any trash that is lying there before setting up anything. Demonstrate by word and example that the wilderness must be kept clean for all to enjoy.

When breaking down camp, be sure to restore the area as closely as possible to its natural appearance. If you cleared sticks and twigs from an area under your tent, return them. Completely douse the fire with water and stir the mixture so that the coals become cold to the touch. If there was a fire ring established before you arrived at the campsite, then leave it. If not, bury the coals, scatter the rocks with the blackened side down, and smooth over the area. Walk through the camp with your children to be sure all signs of your visit are removed and that all litter, yours or not, is carried out. Pack out all bite-sized bits of food in the sump hole and fill in the hole. Finally, fill in the latrine and be sure any bits of remaining toilet paper are either burned or packed out.

An excellent way to instill environmental concern in your children is to ask them to describe the camp as it appears before you set up. Have them walk the chosen camp area with a notebook and write down what they observe. Then, when you are getting ready to leave, have them supervise and help you return the camp to its original appearance. The appearance of the camp area should be as good if not better than the description of the area that they recorded in their notebooks earlier. As you, and they, will find, there is always going to be an impact on the land—primarily traffic lanes. Perhaps this will help to foster a growing conviction that we must all take responsibility for our earth.

BASIC COOKING TIPS AND INFORMATION

FIRE OR STOVE

The fire or stove must be the center of attention in every kitchen. A 360-degree clearance of five feet or more should be created around the cooking area. This area of clearance is kept free from running or playing, stray pieces of equipment, unneeded food, and wood. Always keep pots and kitchen utensils in one place, and nearby, so that the cook will have easy access. Organize food and spices near the kitchen utensils so everything needed for the meal is readily at hand.

There are some basic and mandatory rules to abide by when around a fire. Always wear shoes because stray embers will burn and can cause a serious foot injury. Always remove pots from a fire when adding ingredients to minimize the risk of burning skin or wasting food. Use pot grabbers with work gloves to remove pots. Nylon will melt easily with a stray ember, so keep nylon clothing, tents, and sleeping gear away from the fire. Polypropylene melts with very low heat. Getting too close to a fire while wearing polypropylene could create a painful situation with liner gloves or underwear melting on the skin—I melted a glove on my hand, and it hurt! *Never* leave a fire unattended—if you leave for any reason, first put it out. Having a fire is a privilege and not a right. If the area appears overcamped and wood is scarce, or if building a fire will permanently scar the land (such as near or above timberline), then opt for a stove.

Although you must be very careful with children around an open flame, it is important to allow them to become involved with building and maintaining the fire. It is crucial that they realize fire building is serious business and not play. If they cannot take fire building seriously and are apt to play around with flaming sticks and so on, then you need to take away their fire-helping privileges.

Children of all ages make excellent wood gatherers, but it is generally not until they reach the age of ten or eleven that they become patient and responsible enough to take on the task of fire building. Once at this age

A hot meal and a few quiet moments are the best way to restore energy after a day on the trail.

they can carefully build a fire using kindling and smaller twigs and gradually add larger sticks to feed the growing flame. By the age of ten or eleven they seem to have developed enough maturity to respect the power of flame—if parents have set the proper example.

COOKING

The first and perhaps most important rule of cooking is never overcook. I do not mean food that is cooked too long, but rather an overabundance of cooked food. Try to plan your food needs as closely as possible. If you do have extra food in the pan after a meal, don't bury it. Doing so attracts bugs, rodents, and other animals that wouldn't ordinarily visit the campsite. In addition, the food does not do an animal's diet any good and, in many cases, does harm. If you have a fire, burn the extra food. Otherwise, pack it out—no exceptions.

Just because you are cooking over a fire or stove is no reason to change your cooking plans. Almost anything that is prepared at home can be prepared outdoors. A backpacking stove or the glowing coals of a fire are similar in function, if not appearance, to an oven range at home. The temperature can be controlled. Always use a low flame with a stove and hot coals with no flame when cooking on a fire. Be sure you have chosen a cooking site that is protected from the wind.

When building a fire, it is best to use wood that is no bigger around than your thumb. This will help create an excellent bed of coals fairly rapidly. Finger-sized wood will burn almost completely and will be much easier to clean up and dispose of afterward than will larger branches that do not burn completely through. During cooking, keep a small fire going at one end of the pit and periodically rake the hot embers toward the pots.

BAKING

Yes, you can bake. Baking on a backpacking stove or over a fire will take some practice, but it is well worth it. The idea is to create a type of Dutch oven using a frying pan and lid. You can use a stove on low flame with a small fire of twigs burning on the lid. I have had more consistent success, however, using a fire. When using a fire, the temperature is critical. If your hand, held about six inches from the bed of embers, feels hot but not uncomfortable, then the fire is ready. Be sure you have a very good supply of hot coals. Place the frying pan on a level bed of embers and then shovel a generous layer on the lid. You will need to check the baking periodically. Brush off the top coals and quickly look inside without letting in cold air. Always keep flames away from the baking site.

Children will have fun baking Bisquick horns if you can stand the mess. Mix six parts Bisquick to one part water. Knead the dough until it is firm but not too sticky. Divide the dough into equal parts and then roll each part into long snakes. Find fairly sturdy sticks about three feet long (don't ever cut green wood for this) and whittle a smooth, six-inch surface on one end. Tightly wrap the dough snakes around the smooth end of each stick and bake over hot coals (not flames) until golden brown. When they are done, the horns should easily slide off each stick leaving a steaming pastry just waiting to be filled with jam or honey.

SIMPLE FOOD PREPARATION HINTS

Powdered and instant mixes do not dissolve well in cold water and sometimes not in boiling water. Create a paste first by stirring one part mix and one part warm water to minimize the lumps. For thickening use one part water to one part flour, Cream of Rice, or instant potatoes.

Cheese tends to become clumped or stringy when added directly to dishes with a watery base, such as stews or soups. It is better to melt the cheese first, then add it to the dish.

Remember that cooking at altitude will affect the time it takes to cook a meal because the air pressure is lower. Additionally, wind and cold temperatures will draw heat away from the stove, so it is important to use a good wind-screen and cook in as sheltered an area as possible.

Burned food can be prevented by cooking on low heat in clean pots and by stirring frequently.

Bland food can be attributed to a lack of salt or other spices, but most usually salt. Salt can easily be overdone, especially if the ingredients you are using are salty themselves. A pinch of salt or salt substitute, however, does tend to bring out the flavor in foods.

Undercooking or overcooking is usually caused by adding ingredients in the wrong order or by poor timing. Always add freeze-dried foods before adding additional rice or pasta. If you are adding thickeners, milk, or cheese to the dish, add them just before the dish is done. Add them too soon and they will burn or stick to the bottom of the pan.

CLEANING UP

Illness and diarrhea from unclean conditions are easily prevented if you adhere to a few rules. Wash your hands before preparing any food. Keep pots and utensils clean. Use hot water to wash pots and utensils after each use—don't leave them lying around dirty. Instead of using a plastic scrubby or Brillo pad, which quickly foul and become a breeding ground for bacteria, try a handful of coarse grass, sand, pine cones, or pine needles. Use boiling water to sterilize your dishes and pots every few days. Sterilize your cooking utensils in a small amount of boiling water before using them each evening—save the water to use for clean-up chores after the meal. Avoid using soap; it is very hard to rinse properly and can leave a film that leads to diarrhea. If food sticks to the bottom of a pan, add boiling water to the pan and let it sit overnight. This usually softens the burned food sufficiently for proper cleaning in the morning. Always wash at least one hundred feet away from the nearest water source. Dump rinse water and tiny food particles into a sump hole under a bush and away from camp; remember to pack out the food when you leave.

ANIMALPROOFING YOUR CAMP

Before going camping you will want to know which animals may or may not frequent your campsite. From kangaroo rats to bears, animals are an inquisitive lot that are likely to take advantage of each and every opportunity for free food. A kangaroo rat gnawing through a pack to reach some nuts inside is not an immediate threat to nearby humans, but the damage to the pack could create real problems.

A bear, on the other hand, rummaging through camp and smelling food in a tent, is going to be very surprised when it encounters humans as well as chocolate or fish. The surprise and resulting screaming and growling can, and has, led to very unfortunate consequences and, in a conflict between bears and unarmed humans, bears always cause the most immediate damage.

If you are going to camp in areas such as the Great Smoky Mountains of Tennessee or Yosemite National Park in California, learn to bearproof yourself. Hanging food well away from camp, leaving no food in packs, and *never* taking food or clothing that smells of food into tents are some of the ways to minimize surprise encounters with a bear.

Wherever you travel, though, you do need to animalproof your gear. If there is no bear hazard and you choose not to hang your food, at the very least you should leave pack pockets open. An eager rodent would just as soon gnaw through fabric to get to food, but it will usually take the easy route if an invitation is left via an open zipper or flap. To ensure you receive no unwanted visitors in your tent, leave all food outside of your sleeping area.

To bearbag food: Toss rope over branch; tie one bag to rope; haul bag up to branch and then tie second bag as high on rope as possible (be sure to leave a loop hanging). Balance both bags side by side; retrieve bags by hooking loop with stick and pulling down.

CAMPSITE ACTIVITIES

There are an infinite number of activities that will interest both you and your children around camp. Read on to chapter 5 for specific activities that teach observation skills and nature awareness. As with any activity, be sure that it adheres to the following guidelines: It must be safe; it must not disturb the wildlife; it must not damage the environment in any way; and it should be fun.

Singing around the campfire is a time-honored tradition. There are several books published by Price Stern Sloan and written by Pamela Beall and Susan Nipp that are useful in this endeavor. The books are *Wee Sing*, *Wee*

Sing and Play, *Wee Sing Silly Songs*, and *Wee Sing around the Campfire*. The books are quite small and easily tucked into a pack.

Star gazing is a fun and informative activity. Unless you can blend in stories of legend and tales of bravery to the galactic formations, however, looking at stars is best reserved for older children. Through stores like The Nature Company you can obtain compact star guides that will help you identify those bright flickers in the sky.

Tree climbing, crawfish hunting, firefly chasing, cloud watching, meadow crawling, hide-and-seek, and many other games flit through the minds of youngsters. No game will hold their interest long, and yet, with a little help, the hours should pass with never a dull moment for anyone.

CHORES

Every camping trip will involve its own set of chores and demands. Setting up camp and breaking it down, laying out sleeping bags, stuffing sleeping bags, cooking, cleaning, hanging food, and so on, are all facts of camping life. Though it may seem easier at times to do everything yourself, children should, and must, be encouraged to do their share of chores. Although the actual time and effort provided by younger children is going to be minimal, setting the precedent of requiring children to help out on tasks is important—if you wish them to help out as they get older.

Use the extra set of little hands to help you roll out the tent, separate the stakes, assemble the poles, even hold up one tent end while you secure the other. Give your child the task of unpacking everyone's sleeping pad and bags and laying them out neatly in the tent. It may take him an incredibly long time, but children seem to universally enjoy this activity, and it is well within their capabilities.

During cooking time, young children should not be playing around the fire or stove. Children love to help with cooking, however, by adding water and mixing ingredients. This can easily be accomplished by setting up an area away from the fire and main food preparation area to minimize the amount of dirt kicked into food and knocked-over pots. It is important for your children to realize that when they are given a cooking task, they need to sit at a designated location under adult supervision until the task is done, then they must move completely away from the cooking area until the food is served.

Younger children often enjoy playing in warm dishwater. This desire can be capitalized on by giving them cups and utensils to clean (no knives) after most of the other pots and pans have been cleaned. Chances are they will enjoy playing and cleaning in the water for quite some time.

Exercise some caution in assigning chores. If a child has had a long, hot day on the trail and is exhausted, it might be best to let him or her rest rather than encouraging participation in setting up the tent or cooking. Your best judgment will rule.

As children get older, they can assume more difficult chores and become more active participants in the camp's day-to-day activities. In all situations, try to create a positive atmosphere and work with your children. The only time I have seen a very negative response to chores by children is when a parent sat on his duff and assigned chores, never once lifting a finger to help. All aspects of wilderness travel, if successful, involve the concept of teamwork.

TIPS IN A NUTSHELL

1. Be creative, use games, and keep patient. Variety and perseverance will get your family through a hike successfully.

2. Take frequent rest breaks—every thirty minutes is average. Be sure that you and your children snack, drink, and rest at every rest opportunity.

3. Don't fall into the habit of using food as a motivational tool—except in a real emergency.

4. Once at camp, establish firm camp boundaries immediately. Children are not to go beyond those boundaries without a parent present.

5. Establish well-defined kitchen, toilet, garbage, and sleeping areas.

6. Teach your children to be environmentally responsible. Waste disposal, personal hygiene, cooking, cleaning, fires, and playing all have a lasting impact on the surrounding camp area—sometimes for years.

7. Always animalproof your gear, your tent, and your camp.

8. Encourage children to do their share of chores. Although smaller children can provide little help and their efforts may require the same or more effort on your part, you are setting a precedent that will encourage participation as they get older.

CHAPTER 5

Learning about Nature

THERE IS A TREMENDOUS amount in nature for you and your children to discover together. Yet, as inquisitive as children naturally are, they will learn much more with your encouragement and example. Your family needn't become entomologists, botanists, or ecologists to appreciate what nature has to offer, but there are some activities and techniques that can make each trip outdoors that much more meaningful.

In this chapter you will learn how to use all your senses to make the most out of each discovery and to show you and your children how to become one with the wilderness. While learned individuals have carefully documented and named most of the plants, insects, and animals you will discover, it is more important to know something for what it truly is and not just for its name. Children really aren't concerned that they are looking at an acorn woodpecker. They are more interested in its shape and size, the sounds it makes, how it flies, its color, and so on. With an older child, part of the joy of discovery will be in learning the bird's name with you by using a guidebook.

Your job as a parent will be to see things through a child's eyes. Learn to look beyond the name and view things with a curious sensitivity that opens your senses to exploration. If you can do this and become really aware of things natural, you will enter into a world of childlike thrill and experience. Is there any better way to relate to your children than that? A coyote's yelp under a moonlit sky, the dart of a mouse among leaves, the sweet aroma of a dew-laden meadow under the morning sun, the iridescence of a trout as it swims in the shallows of a mountain brook are moments missed by the unaware.

Taking time to smell scents, keeping your eyes and ears open, and thrilling to each discovery you and your child make will create an opportunity for all of you to become aware of your surroundings in a way never imagined. In a manner of speaking, you and your family will become amateur naturalists.

To put together a "discovery kit" for your children you will need a small nylon stuff sack into which you will put the following items: hand-held magnifying glass; several bandanas; several small, unbreakable, clear plastic specimen containers; aquarium net; small notebook and pencil; set of colored pencils; and several sheets of tracing paper. If you wish, you can easily create an underwater viewer using a large coffee can with both ends removed. Over one end, stretch clear plastic wrap and secure it in place with a rubber band. Now, when you place the plastic-covered end into the water, you will be able to view more clearly the underwater world in a stream or pond.

The most important concept that your children should learn is to never remove anything from its natural environment. With an adult's supervision, it is okay to pick up and examine a small bug, lizard, or even a frog or two, but keep contact to a minimum and always return the animals to where you found them. This is where the clear plastic specimen containers come in handy. When examining a bug or small lizard, gently place it in the container and then look at it through the magnifying glass. This will help minimize the stress of being held in a human hand for any length of time. Always keep captivity to a minimum—longer than one minute is pushing it. If your children learn respect for each creature in the wilderness, they have learned one of the most important lessons of all.

IN THE BACKYARD

The backyard is an excellent place to begin teaching children more about plants and animals. Building bird feeders and creating a wild garden in one corner of the yard are both excellent ways to bring a wilderness feel to an urban environment.

Children should be encouraged to stop and examine the natural world around them.

Bird feeders are more than elaborate trays or concrete dishes on a pedestal and filled with seed. In order to attract the widest variety of birds, you must create a wide variety of feeders. Hummingbird feeding tubes filled with red sugar water, several dishes of seed on the ground near dense bushes, and perhaps one or two feeding platforms elevated on four-by-fours offer an excellent blend. Don't forget to also provide a water source for the birds. The ideal backyard situation will allow for some dense bushes and shrubbery so birds have a perch after and during feeding. Birds seem to feel more protected and secure this way and are more apt to frequent your yard and perhaps nest there, too. Once you begin feeding the birds, don't stop. They will become dependent on the food you and your child are providing and could starve if you suddenly stopped putting seed in the feeding stations.

If at all possible, put as many of the feeders within view and close proximity of a window as you can. This will allow you and your children to observe birds without disturbing them. Keep a pair of binoculars and an identification book near the window for quick and easy access.

Using your imagination, a wild garden that doesn't violate any city ordinances is not too difficult to create. With the addition of a few rocks, perhaps a small artificial pond, and some carefully selected wild flowers and plants, a corner of your yard can be turned into a mini-wilderness that many forms of wildlife will find attractive.

Observation skills and heightening the acuity of a child's senses is important. Show them that they have more than eyes with which to "see" the environment. It is through the initial experiences in a backyard or park that your children will realize that nature is all around them—under the blades of grass, behind the pile of bricks in the yard's corner, in the branches overhead, and in the eaves of the garage.

SPECIAL GAMES FOR THE BACKYARD

Backyard Crawl: The object of this exercise is to teach your children to move slowly and alertly through their environment. Show them how to peer into branches, pull back blades of grass, and examine an overturned stone. Every move is methodical, and children should be encouraged to scan all around them while they crawl across the yard. They should repeatedly look side-to-side, above, below, and behind—almost like an animal that is trying to stay alert to danger and food.

Limited Vision: The object of this exercise is to show children what it is like to look at the world through the eyes of animals. You can do this quite simply by cutting toilet paper tubes in half and then taping them to each lens of an old pair of sunglasses. Obscure peripheral vision with tape so that, when the glasses are in place, the only source of light is through each eye tube. Then have your children walk around discovering a new perspective of their backyard. If you wish to get more technical, Dragonfly Eye Brimfield lenses are available through The Nature Company for around $11. These glasses offer your child a look at the world through compound eyes, much like a bug sees things. Either system obscures vision and should only be used under adult supervision and in a relatively clear area free from dangerous obstacles.

Observation Plot: With your child, mark off a two-foot-by-two-foot square in the yard. Put stakes in each corner and then, with a single length of string fastened to each stake, create a permanent, definable boundary. This little square is your child's to watch and observe from day to day and season to season. Have him or her keep a notebook of what is observed. What happens to the plants? What kind of insects or animals live there? What animals or insects just pass through? What is the earth like? How much sun does the area get? How much rain? How do the sun and rain affect the area? The list of questions is endless and the involvement of your child in the area is limited only by his or her curiosity and your encouragement.

Nightworld Vigil: Going on a night walk with your children is a wonderful experience not to be missed. It can, however, be a somewhat nervous and frightening experience for first timers, so it is best enjoyed if a little forethought and preparation have gone into the adventure. Pick a night that is going to be clear with no moon. Turn out all the lights in the house so there is a minimum of artificial light illuminating the backyard. With a flashlight, walk into the backyard and sit down under a tree or somewhere that is comfortable. Bring a blanket if you wish. With the flashlight on, show your child that although it seems lighter with the flashlight, your vision is really limited to the beam of the light. Now, turn off the light and sit quietly. Explain and talk about each sound you hear—be it a dog barking, a bat flitting through the air, a siren, or a mouse rustling in the compost pile. Begin to help your child distinguish between those sounds that are heard in the day and those heard at night. Ask him why some animals only come out at night and what makes them different from daytime animals? How does the backyard seem different in the dark and why? When the time seems right, walk back to the house without the flashlights. Point out to your child how much better your vision is without the light.

Wilderness with Children

HEAD TO THE PARK

Hug a Tree: This is an excellent exercise that teaches your children to tap into their perceptual skills. Blindfold your child and lead him or her to a nearby tree. Have your child get to really know the tree by hugging, touching, smelling, tasting, and listening to it. Ask him or her to describe the tree to you: its size, age, and shape. Once your child feels that he really knows the tree, lead him away, spin him around, and remove the blindfold. Once removed, ask your child to find his or her tree. Children will discover that it requires all their senses to do this and that it is possible to "see" and "know" an object without using their eyes. Be a participant in this one, too—let your child blindfold you and lead you through the exercise.

Stream Walk: One of my favorite exercises. Be sure that everyone is wearing old tennis shoes and that the day is warm. Beware of slippery rocks, sharp sticks and other objects, poisonous snakes, and hypothermia. Do not stay in the cold water too long. Bring along magnifying glasses, aquarium nets, and either several face masks, clear plastic dishes about six inches across, or your homemade underwater-viewing can. Pick a section of stream that is not too difficult to navigate through, not too long with easy exit points, and not too deep. The idea is to wade down the middle of the stream slowly and methodically. Look for minnows, frogs, tadpoles, crawfish, and so on. Use the net to scoop up what you see and look at your finds in the dishes. Use your masks or place the dishes in the water for a glass-window view of the stream below the surface. Romp, play, and get dirty. Wallow in mud holes and explore every nook and cranny. If you come upon a still pool, have your children stand quietly, observing the world below them through masks or the glass dishes. If they are able to stand quietly for longer than a minute, they will get a peek at another dimension or world swimming around their legs.

Swamp Mucking: A variation on the stream walk with one major difference—you get very muddy. Talk about immersing yourself in nature! When I led groups into the swamp at camp, squeals of happiness and curiosity overcame the nervous apprehensions of things slimy and gross. The idea is to crawl through the swamp following open waterways and ani-

Nikki dabbles her hand in algae floating on a pond while Karen helps her look for frogs.

mal paths. Use obvious caution before diving into a swamp that might be home to alligators, water moccasins, leeches, or snapping turtles.

Fox and the Hare: This game will go a long way in teaching your children to become aware of their surroundings, so that they are able to follow the trail of something because of the signs it leaves. Begin by designating the hare, usually one parent, and the foxes, usually the children and another parent for supervision. Initially, the hare should get a two- to five-minute head start, enough that the foxes lose sight of the hare. The hare will leave signs for the foxes to follow, such as bits of colored paper on the ground or in branches—not too obvious, yet distinct enough to be followed with minimal effort. As the children gain more experience, the hare should get a longer head start and should begin leaving bits of paper that more closely match the color of the terrain. As a variation, the hare can drag a branch behind him to leave a more subtle trail for the foxes to follow. The goal of the game is for the foxes to successfully follow the trail of the hare and catch him.

Blind Trust: This will teach your child to listen carefully to directions as well as learn to use his other senses. It will also teach him important communication and leadership skills. You will want to play this game in a wooded area with some small hills and narrow gullies or other obstacles. Blindfold all in the group except the designated leader. The first time this is played, the designated leader should be an adult. The idea is for the leader to guide the group through the woods going over, around, and under obstacles using only voice commands to give directions. At no time is the leader allowed to move obstacles or touch the players. I recommend that a parent or other adult always keep a watchful eye on the group to maintain a margin of safety. I once had a child try to lead his group over a gully using a narrow log as a bridge. The ten-foot fall that could have resulted was not my idea of a good learning experience.

Snapshot Opportunity: This game is great fun and can be played anywhere. It will teach children to use their observation skills efficiently and accurately. One person needs to be the camera or lens, and the other person needs to work the shutter or picture-taking button. The person guiding the "camera" should search for beautiful, interesting, or creative images. He or she should then set up the camera, who must keep eyes closed until told otherwise, so that a photograph can be taken. The camera guide taps the camera on the shoulder or hand. At this signal the camera opens his eyes, without moving or twisting about, and stares at the image in front of him. After about five seconds the camera guide taps on the shoulder or hand of the camera again and the camera closes his eyes. Allow your child to be the "photographer," using you as the camera, and you will be afforded a unique and, quite possibly, very moving look at what your child views as fascinating and beautiful.

Barefoot in the Woods: Going barefoot is a most natural, and yet rarely enjoyed, experience. To go barefoot encourages a person to slow down, feel the ground underfoot, and relive an almost primeval instinct. Be sure that the ground is free of sharp rocks, thorns, and yes, even glass. Lead your youngsters through the woods single file. Teach them to stalk—to walk as if hunting—through the trees. To do this take a very small and very careful step forward to the outside ball of your descending foot. Very slowly, and without weighting it, roll the foot to the inside of the ball. If nothing that may break with a loud snap or pop is felt underfoot, carefully lower the heel and then fully weight the foot. If your child becomes adept at this, he or she will be able to sneak up closely to birds and animals without spooking them. The key is slow and steady movements.

Stalking can be practiced by having one person, the prey, sit with their eyes closed at one end of a clearing about twenty-five feet wide. Everyone else tries to stalk the person without being heard. If the prey hears a sound he points to it and opens his eyes. If the stalker is able to freeze and not move while the prey is watching, then the game continues. If, however, the prey opens his or her eyes after pointing and the stalker moves at all, even a flinch, the stalker becomes the prey.

World Above or World Below: This activity is a quiet, observational game, which will only work if your children are feeling calm and not overly agitated. It can be played anywhere and is only limited by imagination. To study the world above, the participants must lie still and quietly on their backs looking up at the world above. I find it is most effective to play this game under a dense canopy of leaves, swirling clouds, or in dense, tall grass. Looking down is, appropriately, the opposite of looking up. Everyone lies on his stomach and watches the world as it passes by his face. Looking down works very well above a stream or lake edge, tide pool, or dense patch of grasses or fallen leaves. I have found it helpful, if the ground is cold or hard, to bring sleeping pads for everyone to lie on.

TIPS IN A NUTSHELL

1. Become more concerned with shape, size, color, texture, sound, smell, and taste than with a name drawn quickly out of a guidebook.

2. Learn to view everything for the first time—as if you were your child.

3. Assemble a discovery kit for your children.

4. Never remove anything from the natural environment and handle animals minimally and carefully.

5. Turn your backyard into an urban wilderness through the creation of a washbasin pond, a wild garden, and several bird feeding stations.

CHAPTER 6

Going Cross-Country Skiing

C ROSS-COUNTRY SKIING, or Nordic ski touring, is great fun with children provided you have a readily accessible refuge from the cold and the terrain you are skiing on is not too difficult. Basing out of a cabin with surrounding meadows laden in snow is ideal.

The skills necessary to stay on your feet and have fun on cross-country skis are quite easily acquired. An increasing number of ski resorts have excellent learn-to-ski programs for families and children. I would heartily recommend that everyone in your family who doesn't know how to cross-country ski take a lesson from a professional. Learning from a family member or close friend can be rewarding, but more often than not this experience ends in frustration for all. What is ideal about Nordic skiing is that everyone can do it and, by teaching your family, you are giving your children an enjoyable lifetime activity.

Equipment for going cross-country skiing, while still less expensive than that for downhill, is increasing in price. You should, however, still be able to purchase waxless skis, a good pair of boots, bindings, and poles for less than $200 for adults and less than $100 for children. Spend some time shopping around. Do not just buy the cheapest equipment you find—you get what you pay for in this sport. Karhu and Fischer make special children's skis and ski packages. Give those a close look.

Many outdoor stores offer excellent rental programs that will allow you an opportunity to test the skis before you buy them. Take full advantage of these "demo" programs.

Always buy waxless skis for children. On the average, the skis should be about a child's height for children five years old or younger. Children six years and older can begin to ski with longer skis—up to twenty centimeters longer than his or her height on average. When in doubt, buy shorter skis because your children will initially be more concerned with gripping than with gliding. Longer skis translate into more glide and less grip; conversely, shorter skis offer great grip but reduced glide. A child who cannot climb up a hill or push around on a gentle grade without slipping backward and falling down is a frustrated child and one who will quickly decide skiing is a waste of time.

Boots for children who are three to five years old should be the same warm and waterproof type they use to play in the snow. These boots can be attached to the ski with a simple strap or cable binding. For school-age children, use a boot and binding system that they can easily manage on their own. Salomon Nordic System (SNS) and New Nordic Norm (NNN) boot and binding systems are easily worked by small fingers and still offer plenty of support for more adventurous skiers. Avoid buying boots with "room to grow." Instead, take advantage of the many ski boot trade-in programs offered by retailers around the nation.

Poles are best avoided for children under the age of five. They're just one more piece of equipment to worry about. Children older than five will want and probably need poles. Poles should be shorter in proportion to height than the adult sizes. Until the child successfully learns to use his or her poles, have the sharp metal tips blunted to avoid possible injuries and accidents.

Pulke sleds are ideal pieces of equipment for the family whose children are too young to ski but want to go along with the family. It is not safe to carry infants and toddlers in backpacks or child carriers on ski tours. Children's legs can get constricted in a pack or child carrier, which can lead to frostbite and hypothermia from reduced circulation. The pulke sled is made of wood or fiberglass and is designed to carry one to three children and/or supplies. The sled is remarkably easy to control because it is towed behind an adult who is wearing a padded waist or shoulder harness. A waterproof cover will keep the tiny passengers dry and protected from the wind.

If children are cold, they are miserable. Layers are far better than single bulky garments. When choosing what to buy, the guidelines are essentially the same as mentioned in chapter 2. Remember that if the child is being towed in a pulke sled, he or she is not generating any warmth by exercising and extra steps must be taken to trap and hold body heat.

Work with many light layers that, depending on need, can be easily removed or added. You will develop a skill of knowing when to adjust the layers depending on a child's mood; he will often get grumpy instead of saying "I'm too hot."

Create a layering system consisting of a polypropylene, silk, or Capilene inner layer; several outer layers of Synchilla, bunting, or wool (I avoid wool because it is scratchy and can provide one more source of worry for the child); and a windproof, waterproof, and breathable outer layer. Above all, avoid cotton—it does nothing but absorb water and freeze.

For the outer layer I recommend a separate top and bottom shell—the rain suit top and bottom that you purchased for backpacking is an ideal choice. The exception would be children between the ages of three and five. For them you will want a one-piece suit with a hood. Children do fall down a lot and the one-piece suit will prevent snow from dumping down their necks and creeping up their backs.

Hats and mittens are critical. The hat should be made from wool with a nonitch lining, or from bunting or Synchilla. Mittens are better than gloves for keeping tiny hands warm. Don't buy them too bulky because it will be difficult to grip poles, snowballs, and other playmates. Buy mittens with a removable waterproof shell. If children are quick to pull off mittens, pin or clip them to the sleeve of the snowsuit or jacket.

If you are going to teach your children to ski, or as you follow up on skills taught in a professional lesson, go easy. Don't attempt to turn your children into skiing experts on the first day. Pick a meadow with a gently rolling area and lots of room to play, and stay together. An excellent way to start, although it seems odd, is to let your children "carpet" ski at home.

When you are skiing as a family, remember that your children cannot glide, turn, and fly downhill as you can. Teach them carefully and slowly, never lecturing, always playing. Let children experiment and "discover" problems that you can help them overcome.

Trying to teach kick-and-glide techniques to a child less than eight years

Pulke sleds are the safest and easiest method of taking children too young to ski along on a family outing.

old is not only ridiculous, it is frustrating. They would much rather be bounding around making snowmen, building igloos, and keeping warm. Let's face it, constantly falling down while getting tangled up in poles and skis is not exactly a rip-roaring good time. Learn to set realistic goals for your children, especially the younger ones.

Children between the ages of four and six are still coping with balance and coordination and have little long-term endurance. Any formal lesson for children of this age should consist of plenty of fun and games with skis and no poles. Tag, dodge ball, soccer using hands to move the ball, and follow the leader are all very effective teaching aids. Children find themselves having a great time on skis while naturally learning to balance and turn. Later on, these basic skills are easily adapted to a longer family outing.

Children of all ages—even adults—fall down a lot; it is a part of learning. Teaching children how to roll onto their backs to untangle skis in the air is an important skill. Follow this by showing them how to place their skis parallel on the downhill side, roll forward onto their knees, and push up from there. This one skill will save hours of exhausting effort and frustration for your children.

Follow the leader is perhaps one of the easiest and most useful techniques to use when helping your children master skis. Leave your poles behind and begin to shuffle around. Lead them on a merry chase, but ever so slowly. Crouch down, stand up, sidestep, waddle, make stars in the snow, play tag, and have fun. As you encounter skills the children want to learn, use visual imagery to communicate important techniques.

"Walking like a duck" is useful when teaching uphill or herringbone technique. "Pretending to drive a car" is useful when teaching proper body positioning for going downhill.

As the children's skills increase and their level of adventure rises, your family will want to head out from the meadow. It is essential that you never lose sight of the fact that is supposed to be fun. Always bring along plenty of water and snacks. It is also a good idea to take extra socks, mittens, a waterproof ground cloth for sitting, lots of sunscreen, and a special hot drink as a surprise.

It is an excellent idea to plan a ski outing with another family. This will provide playmates for the kids and an opportunity for parents to take shifts watching the children.

TIPS IN A NUTSHELL

1. Buy children's skis too short rather than too long. Do not buy boots too large—instead take advantage of ski-retailer boot trade-in programs.

2. Get professional lessons. When skiing with younger children who are just learning the sport, play lots of games. Tag, fox and the hare, and follow the leader are great fun. Remember to ski slowly and allow the children to win frequently.

3. Keep ski-tour length within the ability of everyone.

4. Pack lots of wholesome snacks, water, and maybe a hot drink. Hot chocolate and warmed cider are big favorites.

5. Take extra socks, mittens, and hats.

6. Plan on bringing another family along. The additional adult supervision will allow time for parents not watching children to be able to ski at a faster pace. The additional children will provide more playmates and entertainment.

7. Remember to take plenty of breaks—pack along strips of Ensolite and/or a ground cloth to sit on in the snow to help everyone stay warm and dry.

CHAPTER 7

Going Canoeing or Kayaking

EXPLORING THE WILDERNESS in a canoe is a unique camping experience for a family. While you will be limited to relatively calm waterways for most exploration, canoe camping presents a smorgasbord of opportunity for fun, safe trips in extremely beautiful surroundings. Canoeing is a very comfortable way to transport yourself and your family with a minimum of effort. It is especially ideal for the family with young children who cannot or are less inclined to walk lengthy distances.

Traveling by boat does have its hazards. Heavy winds can quickly whip up waves that could overturn a canoe or kayak. A gentle river could surprise the paddler with unannounced rapids around a distant bend. Whatever the cause, it is enough to realize that no parent should take his or her children on the water without acquiring basic paddling skills and safety knowledge. Classes, clubs, and various demonstration days sponsored by manufacturers are excellent sources of information and instruction.

I also recommend that your children be able to float and tread water comfortably before you take them on a lake or river. There are many lessons offered by organizations such as the YMCA that help to drown-proof babies and children as young as two years old. Inquire at a local community pool for information.

Buying a canoe or kayak and the accompanying gear can be somewhat expensive and a tad confusing. Choosing what type of boat you want for your family is a highly individual decision. There is no canoe or kayak that will work well under all circumstances.

Will you be using the boat on flat or whitewater? Will you be paddling rivers or lakes? How much weight and gear do you want the canoe or kayak to hold? How durable does it need to be? How much can you afford to spend? All of these questions need to be answered before deciding on your purchase. Although a canoe or kayak purchase is expensive, it is an item that can last a lifetime with proper care.

If buying is a little out of your family budget this year, that's okay. Many marinas, river and ocean outfitters, and some retail outlets provide rental packages at a relatively reasonable rate. Most will require you to demonstrate some level of competency in the craft or take a lesson from them before letting you out on the open water.

There are many safety considerations before embarking on a paddle trip, but none so important as wearing life jackets. Every person in the boat, even the smallest of children, must wear a Coast Guard-approved life preserver. These preservers should be designed so that they will keep a person floating upright and tilted slightly back with the face supported out of the water—even if the person is unconscious.

If you have any doubts about the effectiveness of a life preserver, have your child or other members of the family hang limp and totally relaxed in a pool while wearing the preserver. If they are not adequately supported by the preserver according to the aforementioned guidelines, the preserver is not safe. You also need to check the preservers' fit and buoyancy as your children grow. What may have fit and supported their weight one year may be inadequate the next.

When dressing for a paddle trip, consider that, when wet, the body will chill quite easily, even in a very slight breeze. While a bathing suit or a T-shirt and shorts are appropriate in warm, sunny weather, always be sure to pack long pants, a warm sweater, wool socks, and a rain suit. In cooler weather layer accordingly, just as you would for cross-country skiing or hiking. Beware of cottons and wools, which become extremely heavy when wet and tend to weigh a person down in the water.

Hats, sunglasses, and strong sunscreen are absolute necessities. The sun's rays can be very intense when reflected off the water and will burn a child's sensitive skin very easily. Don't forget to reapply sunscreen after swimming, and don't forget to apply it under the ears and ear lobes, under the chin, and under the nose—in a reflected sun those areas are often overlooked and burn easily.

Footwear is a tricky item. Tennis shoes work well in warm water and weather, but feet will chill easily if the water is cold or the weather turns cool. If the shoes are big enough, putting on a pair of wool socks will help. Always pack an extra pair of shoes for everyone to wear when on shore. Hiking around in wet shoes is both uncomfortable and potentially dangerous—wet shoes and slippery rocks can be a bruising combination. Old tennis shoes with holes in them for drainage make great water play shoes. Because of the possibility of sharp rocks or sticks in a water area, I recommend that children always wear shoes when playing in the water.

Some companies do make neoprene booties, rather like divers wear, in smaller sizes with soles for walking. These are super because they keep feet warm when wet, are light, and are easily slipped on. The drawback is that they keep the feet continually wet. There are other types of boating footwear or paddling shoes similar to slippers on the market that seem to work very well. Sandals, such as Tevas, are also good and can be worn with a warm pair of wool socks for insulation. Check with your local outfitter and buy what seems to best meet your family's needs and budget.

Keeping your gear dry when boating is a serious concern. It is no fun, after paddling for several hours and arriving at the campsite just before dusk, to find your sleeping bags are soaked because they were sitting in the bottom of the canoe. Canoe outfitters and retail stores offer a variety of bags made of heavily waterproofed nylon with leakproof seals that won't let water in even if all your gear gets dumped in the river.

For smaller items such as cameras, books, and so on, army-surplus ammunition cans work outstandingly well. I have several that have been painted orange for visibility (easier to spot floating in a river than army green) and lined with old Ensolite for padding my camera gear. The ammunition cans have been subjected to many a rapid while whitewater rafting, and my cameras and notebooks have never suffered a drop of water.

Because children seem to enjoy boating, and because you can pack along a large camp stove, kitchen, and lots of fresh food in a cooler, canoeing does seem to be a perfect opportunity to go camping with children. It is

Wilderness with Children

Canoeing is a fun and easy way for the whole family to enjoy an outdoor adventure together. Photo by Bill Byrne.

not without its drawbacks, however, if certain considerations are not taken into account.

Children are naturally active. The younger the child, the shorter the attention span, and the less amount of time he will be able to sit anywhere quietly. Don't plan on driving for a long period of time and then expect the child to sit quietly in the boat for several more hours while you paddle around. A certain amount of activity and entertainment is necessary to keep him happy while on the water.

Try, if at all possible, to keep the driving distance to and from the boating destination to a minimum. Two to three hours is about the most any parent can expect of a child without a break. Once you get to the boat launch site, take some time to play tag, toss a ball, or engage in some other activity. Don't just unload the car, load the boat, and head out.

Once on the water, keeping a child entertained and interested is not too difficult. Just as with backpacking or hiking, activity ideas need to be creative and varied—nothing will work forever or all the time. With smaller children it is a great idea to give them a tiny paddle that they can dip in and out of the water. Although their paddling will be ineffective, it will not hamper the adult's paddling efforts, and it will make the children feel like an important and active part of the excursion.

Many youngsters like to fish. Although this activity will usually only work if the parents like to fish as well, giving a child a fishing pole to use as you float along is great fun for them. Who knows, they may even catch the evening's dinner! Whether they catch anything isn't the point, however. As any learned fisherman will tell you: "It's the fishin' that's important, not the catchin'."

Staying as close to shore as is safely allowed is a great way to keep a child interested. This way there will be lots of sandbars, undercut banks, and marshy areas for them to look at as you pass. There is also an increased possibility of spotting wildlife on the nearer banks or beaches. Imagine your child's amazement as you quietly slip by a large moose chewing river grasses, water dripping from its muzzle and weeds hanging from its antlers.

Be sure to plan on plenty of shore breaks; one every thirty minutes is perfect. Children will not benefit from all-day paddling grinds to reach the ideal campsite. Just as you spent time playing on shore between the car and loading the boat, you will need similar time during a day-long paddle trip.

TIPS IN A NUTSHELL

1. Never venture out on a lake or river without first acquiring basic paddling skills.

2. Everyone in the boat must wear a Coast Guard-approved life preserver. Be sure that each preserver floats the wearer with the feet down and face out of the water.

3. Dress warmly and in layers. Pack along extra clothing that everyone can change into if they get soaked.

4. Always apply generous amounts of sunscreen—don't forget the ear lobes, tip of the nose, and under the chin.

5. Footwear should be worn at all times, even in the water. Old tennis shoes with holes work well, as do specially made paddling shoes and sandals.

6. Use leakproof bags and ammunition cans to keep valuables dry.

7. Keep driving distances to and from the boating site to a minimum. Any longer than two or three hours means children will get agitated if they sit for any length of time in a boat.

8. Keep a child entertained by boating near the shore, giving them a small paddle, setting them up with a fishing pole, and so on.

9. Take plenty of shore breaks.

CHAPTER 8

Going Biking

B ICYCLE TOURING WITH CHILDREN can be easily accomplished at any age. Mountain biking, on the other hand, is best suited to older children. Riding a mountain bike requires a strong sense of balance, agility, concentration, and a certain amount of stamina—something children less than the age of ten are not automatically blessed with. Bicycling in general is a very adaptable sport, however. Paved bike paths, smooth dirt roads, and bike lanes on certain roads all provide an experience suitable for the family.

Whatever type of bicycling you have in mind for the family, there are some general considerations that apply. When choosing a bike for your child, do not overlook the length of the crank—the arm from the chainwheel to the pedal. Most bike shops fit adults and children alike by having them straddle the frame with both feet flat on the ground. It is true that there should be at least an inch of clearance between the crotch and the top tube (two to three inches in mountain bikes). With smaller children, however, even if the frame fits, if the crank is too long, they will end up struggling to reach the pedals on the downstroke and risk smacking the handlebar with their knee on the way up. Does that sound like fun to you? Make sure the bike you purchase has a reasonable length crank for your child.

The best style of multipurpose bike to purchase for younger children is a BMX (bicycle motocross). Numerous manufacturers make them. Be sure that what you get is sturdy. Up to the age of ten, your child is best served by a single-speed bike. As your youngster's hands become larger and stronger, a more sophisticated ten-speed or mountain bike will be appropriate. Fat tires are more stable and versatile for children than are thin ones. Stay away from banana-style seats because they tend to distribute the child's weight unevenly over the bike and interfere with balance.

Wilderness with Children

Helmets for everyone in the family are mandatory. After your child reaches the age of five, the head usually stops growing in size, so a helmet purchased at this age can reasonably be expected to last until the child is about ten. Some children are a bit stubborn about wearing a helmet. Up until the time a child's head stops growing, purchase a helmet with a certain amount of growth adjustment. In most cases children will follow a parent's lead, so put your helmet on first and your child is likely to follow. If not, then get off the bike and the trip is over. Under no circumstances should you allow your child to ride without a helmet.

Children under the age of seven will most likely be unable to pedal their own bike alongside parents for any length of time—certainly not much more than on a neighborhood tour. With smaller children you must decide between a bicycle seat and a trailer. Choose a seat that is made of sturdy plastic with a high back rest, arm rests, spoke protectors, seat belts, and a chest harness. Seats will fit a child comfortably up to the age of four, but after that either they must pedal on their own bike or you will need to consider purchasing a trailer. When carrying a child in the seat, be sure to watch your speed and control. This is important not only for your child's safety, but for your safety and comfort as well. Be sure to provide head support that will ensure a more comfortable ride should the child fall asleep.

Trailers, although somewhat expensive, are a safe and stable alternative to bike seats and the only way to go when a child is too old to play child-seat jockey but too young to pedal. There are several different styles on the market so spend your time choosing carefully. Should the children face forward or back? Should the trailer be of plastic or aluminum? Do you want a roof for weather protection? Do you want the trailer to attach at the frame or near the seat (the frame attachment allows the bike to fall without tipping the cart)?

Once you have assembled and attached the bike trailer, be sure to make it extremely visible to drivers by attaching an orange safety flag on a six-foot wand attached at the road-side rear corner of the trailer.

With only one child there is room in the trailer to carry camping gear, which reduces the pannier load and rear wheel drag considerably. Trailers can haul up to one hundred pounds of gear without too much difficulty or strain for the pedaler.

Before heading out on your first trip with a trailer or child seat, get thoroughly used to pedaling with the extra weight. This is especially true if you are planning a family bike camping trip and the bikes are also loaded with panniers. Extra weight will affect the way a bike rides and its stability. Braking takes longer, hills seems steeper, and corners must be taken more carefully.

As your children get older, they will become skilled and strong enough to venture out with you on longer tours. It is crucial that they firmly understand the rules of the road and can positively control their bike—even if you are just riding off road. Ride with traffic; stop before entering a street from a driveway, parking lot, alley, or sidewalk; stop at all stop signs and lights; look over the shoulder and wait for overtaking traffic before turning left; avoid oncoming traffic; and no playing around in the road.

Dogs are an often talked about fear for people on bikes. I have had very few bad experiences with dogs, but it is wise to be prepared in any case. Sprays, loud horns, clubs, and so on are not a good course of action when being chased by a dog; quite often these methods only anger the dog. The best solution is to dismount from the bike and walk. This will give the dog a chance to see you as a human. With careful scooting and leaping you should be able to keep the bike between you and even the most unfriendly beast. If dismounting fails to work, then I would resort to using a spray repellent in the dog's face or a sharp whack over the snout with your tire pump.

Always take plenty of water, a tire pump, first-aid kit, a small tool kit, a spare tube, tire-patch kit, snacks, and extra clothing. I also advise wearing bike gloves to pad and protect your hands.

There is a wide variety of specialized clothing on the market for bikers, but much of it is not necessary. Bike shorts and bike shoes are well worth the investment, however. The well-dressed rider wears cycling gloves, riding shorts, stiff-soled riding shoes, sunglasses, helmet, and a T-shirt. For weather changes you should also carry a windbreaker and thermal underwear.

Using a special trailer, you can safely and easily pull your child and gear along. Photo by Mark Lord.

TIPS IN A NUTSHELL

1. Be sure the crank length on your child's bike is appropriate.

2. Everyone must wear a helmet at all times. A good pair of bike shorts and riding gloves are also recommended.

3. Before riding with a child seat or a trailer, practice pedaling with the added weight and drag. Your turning and stopping abilities will be different.

4. Head support for your child will help ensure a more comfortable ride when he or she inevitably falls asleep and the head goes limp.

5. Be sure that your children understand and practice safe road rules before they are allowed to pedal along on any outing.

6. Pack along a compact bike-repair kit, water, snacks, first-aid kit, tire pump, and tire-patch kit.

7. Bring a windbreaker and some warm clothes in the event the weather changes.

CHAPTER 9

First Aid and Safety

T HE BEST FIRST AID IS prevention. Just as you would spend time teaching your children to say no to drugs and to be cautious of strangers, you should spend time teaching them outdoor safety. Although teaching children safety in the outdoors is potentially tricky (you don't want to scare them out of the wilderness), it is important to be honest and frank.

Teaching children to be cautious around fire, sharp objects, and camp hazards, such as guy lines, is fairly basic but important. There are, however, more subtle hazards that children should know how to identify.

SAFETY CONCERNS

ROCKS, RUBBLE, BRUSH PILES, AND FALLEN LOGS

Loose rocks could give way and cause a slip and a sprained ankle. Rocks can also slide to create a much more dangerous situation. Rubble, brush piles, and logs can give way when weight is placed on them and lead to open wounds, broken bones, and bruises. It is also possible for supports to give way and shift, trapping the unfortunate victim. Children love to climb on fallen logs—so do adults—but caution is important. Loose bark, moss, and debris can all lead to a nasty fall.

I know everyone has heard the phrase "Put that down or you will put someone's eye out!" Protecting the face when travelling through dense underbrush, walking at a safe distance behind the person ahead, and taking care that branches do not snap back in someone's face do much toward preventing an eye injury.

TREES
Climbing trees is great fun, but care must be exercised. Teach children to look for weak or dead branches that might break under their weight. Some trees have moss growing on their branches that could cause an untimely slip. Never break branches or try to pull branches out of trees for firewood. (The only exception is in an emergency.) It is not an environmentally sound practice, and it invites potential injury by pulling the tree down or causing an avalanche of broken branches to follow.

WATER, MUD, WET SAND, AND RIVERBANKS
Water attracts children like ants to a picnic. Children should be instructed not to go near water except where it is slow moving and very shallow. And they should never go in the water without adult supervision. Even there, potential hazards exist that must be identified. Mud and wet sand on a riverbank or lake edge is sometimes quite deep. A headlong sprint to the water without first checking the mud or sand could result in a child becoming stuck, making rescue very difficult.

Riverbanks are notorious for giving way without notice. Teach your children the dangers of sitting or standing on the edge of high riverbanks, which may be undercut by the water flow. Also teach them that anytime the water is moving swiftly, the riverbanks are suspect. Should a riverbank give way and pitch a child into rapids or cold, deep water, you have a potential drowning situation or the possibility for severe hypothermia.

SNOW AND ICE
Snow and ice present another range of hazardous possibilities. It is important to teach your children to stay alert in snowy and icy conditions. Snow-covered trees and rock ledges and ice overhangs can give way without notice, burying whatever, or whomever, is underneath. Snow at the top of ravines or on ridges has the potential to slide or avalanche. Snow also melts into clothing, causing chilling and the potential for hypothermia. Ice is deceptive. Stay away from ice-covered lakes, rivers, riverbanks, ponds, and

so on. There really is no safe way to determine absolute strength of the ice, and a fall through the ice into the water below can be deadly.

POISONOUS PLANTS
The major worry with older children will typically be poison oak, poison ivy, or poison sumac. Not all these plants grow in every area of the United States, so you should check with your local park service to see which plants are where. Children should know how to identify leaf clusters and color so they can avoid the nasty skin reaction to these plants. With younger children you must also teach them not to taste test. Berries, mushrooms, and leaves are all inviting to young eyes and palates and could cause potential poisoning accidents.

ANIMALS AND INSECTS
While it is important to educate your children about the risks of poisonous animals, insects, and other animal hazards, it is not appropriate to terrorize them. Instill caution and respect, not fear. When talking to your children about various animals, educate them with the fullest picture that you can provide; sometimes this may require a bit of research on your part, either alone or with your child. To say that bears are dangerous and nothing else is not in the best interest of your child—or the bear. Children should learn all the outdoors has to offer—as much as you are able to share. You may even find yourself having to de-Hollywood their images of animals. Read books together at home, go to museums and zoos, and do anything you can to present the most complete picture possible.

The more your child learns, and you too for that matter, the more he will be able to appreciate the outdoors, the animals that live there, and the behaviors necessary to coexist in that environment safely. If you and your children are aware and alert, then you will rarely encounter a situation where you are bothered by a dangerous animal.

FIRST AID

The information provided in this chapter on first-aid materials and procedures is not a substitute for trained medical assistance in an emergency.

An appropriately stocked first-aid kit is essential no matter how short the hike or adventure.

Whenever possible, seek medical help. A first-aid kit doesn't help anyone if it is in the hands of an untrained person—in fact more harm can be caused than good! Improper or inappropriate administering of drugs or failure to recognize immediate requirements causes needless injuries and deaths every year. *Everyone in your family should become trained in first aid and cardiopulmonary resuscitation (CPR).* Excellent programs are offered through the Red Cross, the American Heart Association, and private organizations or hospitals. Frequently organizations such as the Sierra Club or other outdoor-oriented groups offer wilderness first-aid courses. Become trained; become safe.

The following information is to be used as a source only and should not be considered a training in first aid or an endorsement of techniques or products. Consult your doctor or local library and become trained and certified in first aid before assembling a first-aid kit and heading out-doors.

Having just said all that, let me put your mind at ease. First aid is the practice of common sense. In my years of teaching wilderness first aid and guiding trips, I have witnessed some of the finest first aid performed by rel-atively untrained individuals. These individuals did not reach into a drug bag and begin administering medicine, nor did they do anything tricky or fancy. What they did was remain calm, provide comfort, and tend to the needs of the injured parties as best they could. That is the essence of first aid—do good if you can, but do no harm.

Before going on any outing with your children, it is important they also become familiar and comfortable with some simple first-aid skills. Should something happen to an adult, children will need to feel confident in their skills and abilities, no matter how basic. Children should never have to feel helpless. Practice in the house, backyard, or nearby park the various skills and situations that will be of use to your children. The more the child knows, the more independently and confidently he or she will act in emer-gency or stressful situations. More important, the child will begin to learn how to prevent injury in the first place.

In all first-aid situations there are basics that govern action for most pro-cedures. First is identifying the method of injury and then ensuring that no one else in the group, including the potential rescuer, will also be injured. Second is to remove the mechanism or situation of injury from the injured party if it is life threatening (for example a rockfall, avalanche, electrical wire, and so on). This may involve moving the injured person, but only if the immediate situation is life threatening and under no other circumstance. Anytime you move anyone, you risk aggravating an injury and causing either permanent damage or even death.

Third, perform the ABCs: Be sure the *Airway* is not blocked or compro-mised in any way; evaluate *Breathing* and observe the rise and fall of the chest; check for *Circulation*—see if the person has a pulse. If the answer is no to any of the above, then you must begin either rescue breathing or CPR. Establishing an airway and CPR can be performed effectively while trans-porting the patient out of immediate danger—don't get caught wasting pre-cious seconds.

Fourth, control any bleeding. Bleeding can be controlled by applying direct pressure to the wound using your hand to hold a dressing in place. A clean article of clothing, a bandana, sanitary napkins, or whatever clean cloth or absorbent material is available will work as a dressing. Add additional dressings to the wound while maintaining pressure until the bleeding is controlled. If the stack of dressings becomes too bulky or ineffective, remove from the top, but do not remove the bandage in direct contact with the wound because you risk restarting the bleeding.

Fifth, stabilize any other injuries, such as fractures and dislocations, to prevent further discomfort and harm. Never try to set a fracture or restore a dislocation. Although this is sometimes done in a wilderness situation, it is done only to save life and only by thoroughly trained personnel. Maintaining a calm and comfortable environment for the injured person while stabilizing injuries is essential.

Sixth, always treat for shock. Shock is a life-threatening situation, even if the injury is not. Shock can be brought on by allergic reaction, by injury, by poisoning, by illness, and even by seeing someone else injured. Some of the classic signs and symptoms of shock are weakness, pale color, cool and/or clammy skin, irregular breathing, nausea, dizziness, and shivering—even in warm weather. It is important to maintain the injured party's temperature. Wrap the person in an emergency blanket, sleeping bag, or extra clothing if cold. In hot weather keep the person cool by creating shade. Always attempt to keep the individual insulated from the ground. As a rule, keep the injured party lying down, comfortable, and resting with the feet raised. In the event of a head injury do not raise the feet. Listen to the injured parties and meet their needs; do not try to restrain them in an attempt to "do what the book says." If they feel more comfortable sitting up, let them. Do, however, continue to encourage them to rest and keep warm.

WATER PURIFICATION

Water purification unfortunately has become a necessary duty regardless of the water's source. A one-time experience with diarrhea and vomiting from impure water is all it will take to be thoroughly convinced. There are several excellent ways to purify water when camping. Boiling is virtually foolproof; it does, however, take a fair amount of time and considerable fuel. Additionally, I have yet to meet an adult or child who enjoys drinking hot water on a hot day.

Purifying with a filter is fairly immediate and renders quite clear and clean-tasting water. There are numerous models on the market that range in price from $20 to $200. If you choose a filter, select one that ensures filtration of giardia; amazingly, not all do. Consider weight and size, too. Remember that you will have to carry whatever you choose. Also remember you are relying on a mechanical device that, like most mechanical devices, has been known to fail. Filters can clog, become jammed, be dropped and crack, or be used improperly, all of which can lead to impure water. I use filters, but I also carry a small bottle of chemical treatment as a backup.

The chemical treatments available are quite easy to use. You have a choice between iodine- and chlorine-based purification. Iodine has worked well for me, and I have been very happy with both Polar Pure and Potable Aqua. Potable Aqua is a tablet system that is easy for children to understand and use, although it does have a very limited shelf life once the bottle is open. Polar Pure has a much longer shelf life and is more versatile, but it may be more complicated to use. Of the chlorine-based systems, the Sierra Water Purifier appears to be the best by most accounts. The method of purification is somewhat involved, though. It also uses a 30 percent solution of hydrogen peroxide to take any residual chlorine taste out of the water, which is a strong solution that will burn skin, so I feel its use around children should be avoided.

ALTITUDE SICKNESS

Altitude sickness is the body's reaction to the lack of available oxygen in the atmosphere. The higher the elevation, the less the oxygen, and the more likely the body is to succumb to altitude sickness. Typically, altitude sickness occurs at eight thousand feet or above, although there have been a few documented occurrences at lower elevations. Signs and symptoms are nausea, headache, shortness of breath, and extreme fatigue. Rest, food, and water are the only cure because the body takes time to acclimate to the higher altitude. Descending a few thousand feet until the person begins to feel better may be the best treatment. The odds of getting altitude sickness can be greatly reduced by drinking water, eating well, and gaining altitude gradually.

High altitude pulmonary edema and high altitude cerebral edema are much more severe reactions to altitude. They require immediate descent and evacuation to a hospital. If the individual develops pneumonialike signs or begins to stagger, becomes incoherent, or suffers unbearable head pressure, evacuate immediately.

BLISTERS

Blisters are caused by friction or constant uncomfortable binding pressure—usually from a poorly fit boot or inadequately protected feet. To minimize the chance of getting foot blisters and assuming your boots fit properly: wear two pairs of socks, one thin liner and a thicker cushion outer sock of wool; take time to remove debris that has fallen into your boot; never hike for extended periods with wet feet.

Should discomfort or a hot spot begin to develop, stop immediately and attend to your feet. If there is evident redness but no blister, apply moleskin directly to the hot spot to take care of the discomfort. If a blister has begun to form, cut a doughnut out of molefoam to surround the blister. Secure this in place with a strip of moleskin, if needed.

If the blister is broken, treat it as an open wound. Clean the area with soap and water, then dress it accordingly. I have found that an application of SecondSkin, a gelatinlike sheet, directly over the broken blister and secured in place with moleskin works well.

You may find that if your feet are dirty and somewhat sweaty, moleskin or adhesive tape will peel off or not adhere well to the skin. You can prevent this by first cleansing the area with an alcohol wipe, then applying tincture of benzoin around, but not on, the wound. This will prepare the skin for an application of adhesive.

BURNS

Minor burns such as those received from a hot stove, a pot handle, or a match are usually not serious enough to warrant medical attention. Treatment, however, should be taken seriously. Immerse the affected part in cool water to alleviate the pain and stop the burning sensation. Clean the area with soap and water and consider the application of a topical anesthetic to minimize pain.

For more severe burns, which blister or have deep tissue damage, the victim will need medical attention.

BRUISES

Bruising is caused by a blow to the muscle or soft tissue, resulting in bleeding into those tissues that, in turn, causes swelling and discoloration. If swelling and pain increase dramatically over a twenty-four hour period, then a visit to the nearest emergency room is a wise precaution. Otherwise, resting the extremity in an elevated position with a cold, but not wet, compress is appropriate.

OPEN WOUNDS: CUTS, LACERATIONS, AND INCISIONS

The best first aid for an open wound is cleansing the area with antibacterial soap and water. Apply a clean, nonadhering dressing, such as a Telfa pad, and secure it with adhesive tape. For serious bleeding, apply direct pressure to the wound with a sterile compress. Elevate the wound above the level of the heart, if necessary, to slow the bleeding. Continue to apply direct pressure and add more compresses to the original dressing until the bleeding slows or stops. When the bleeding has stopped, secure the wound with a compression bandage and head to the hospital for stitches.

If stitches become necessary, they must be placed within six hours after the wound has occurred to be effective and to minimize scarring. Do not allow the wound to get too old or too dirty. Steristrips or butterfly bandages can be used as an interim stitch to hold incisions or lacerations together until stitches can be used. The wound must be clean and antiseptic before using Steristrips if at all possible.

It is appropriate to apply an antibacterial ointment to the dressing before applying it to the wound. This will help prevent infection, and infection is a major concern for all wounds. Puncture wounds and abrasions are the most likely to become infected because of minimal bleeding and dirt deeply introduced or ground into the wound. Lacerations create a fair amount of torn and dead skin and are also very likely to become infected. Always clean a wound with soap and water.

EYES

Should any chemical, such as stove fuel, chlorine, or other contaminants, get in the eye, flush with large amounts of water. Be sure to flush from the inside corner of the eye (nearest the bridge of the nose) out, so you don't flood the face or other eye with contaminant. Keep irrigating for approximately ten to fifteen minutes until you are sure the chemical has been removed. Use a continuous gentle stream of water and not a blast, such as from a garden hose. After irrigating the eye, remove any coagulated chemical from the eye with a moistened cloth. Irrigate the eye again. Do not put medications in the eye. Cover the injured eye with a sterile gauze pad and immediately take that person to the hospital.

In the case of a puncture wound, do not remove the object if it is still in the eye. Create a doughnut bandage from a bandana and place it around the injured eye. This will provide a raised protective surface against which you can bandage the eye without risk of pushing on the object. You will need to bandage both eyes so the injured party is not tempted to move the eyes around and cause greater pain and damage. Evacuate to a hospital immediately.

IMPALED OBJECTS
Probably the most common item impaled is a fishhook. If a fishhook becomes stuck in a finger or elsewhere, you need to push the hook's barbed end all the way through the skin, clip it off, and then pull the shaft back through. This is very painful, and it sometimes helps if you deaden the area with lidocaine or ice. If at all possible, this procedure should be performed in an emergency room.

HEAT EXHAUSTION, HEAT STROKE, AND HEAT CRAMPS
Heat exhaustion is caused by the body's loss of important fluids and salt, usually in a hot environment. This can be prevented by eating correctly, drinking two to four quarts of fluid per day, reducing physical activity during very hot weather, and perhaps adding an electrolyte supplement to your drinking water such as ERG, BodyFuel, or a similar substance. The signs and symptoms are dizziness, pale skin, restlessness, nausea, rapid heartbeat, and headache. Treat by removing the heat source—taking off clothing, getting into shade, and so on. Sponge the victim down with water. Give sips of fluid fortified with an electrolyte supplement or salt. Be careful that in initiating the cooling process, you don't send the victim into hypothermia.

Heat stroke is far more dangerous than heat exhaustion, and its onset is much more sudden. Confusion, irrational behavior, rapid pulse and respirations, hot and dry skin, and unconsciousness are common symptoms. To treat, clothing should be removed and the body moistened with cool water and fanned to increase air circulation and evaporative cooling. Again, do not cool the body into a hypothermic state. Evacuation to a hospital is necessary.

Heat cramps are most often caused by a dilution of the salt in the body fluids. Usually this is due to heavily worked muscle activity and an intake of excessive water without accompanying salt. Drinking fluid fortified with electrolytes will help prevent this painful problem. If a cramp should occur, it can be massaged and stretched. Muscle soreness is likely for several days after a cramp.

HYPOTHERMIA AND FROSTBITE

Hypothermia is caused by the body's inability to generate enough heat to compensate for heat loss. The difference between mild and severe hypothermia is very difficult to recognize unless you have a thermometer that reads below 94 degrees Fahrenheit. Hypothermia is very difficult to treat and is much easier to prevent. Eating a balanced diet; drinking adequate amounts of fluid; dressing appropriately for the weather; keeping your body and clothing dry by controlling sweat and preventing outside moisture from seeping in; covering your head, neck, and hands; and wearing clothes that will maintain insulative properties—even when wet—are all ways to prevent hypothermia. Wet clothing, sitting on snow, and a cold wind across a body moist with perspiration are all ways to become hypothermic.

A mildly hypothermic person will complain of cold, may have difficulty performing simple motor functions, may become apathetic, perhaps will be shivering, and will have a body-core temperature down to 95 degrees. Move them from the cold into a warm environment, remove damp clothing or add warm insulation, and offer warm liquids and food if the victim is fully conscious and able to swallow easily.

For moderate to severe hypothermia the victim will exhibit signs and symptoms such as slurred speech, stumbling, unresponsiveness, decreased pulse and respiration, mental confusion, and unconsciousness. The body core temperature will be below 95 degrees Fahrenheit. End the exposure immediately by covering the victim. Do not allow the victim to walk or move, and handle the victim very gently. Movement may force cold blood from the limbs into the core of the body and further complicate the situation.

Check the victim for signs of frostbite. If you cannot get the victim to a hospital quickly, then rewarming may be appropriate. Focus on applying warmth to the head, neck, armpits, and groin. Heat will most easily reach the body core from these areas. Use warm water bottles, warm blankets, or other warm bodies. Take great care that you do not burn the victim. In all situations of potential hypothermia, believe the signs and symptoms even if the victim doesn't.

Frostbite is caused when circulation is restricted or stopped to the extremities such as fingers and toes. This reduction in circulation allows the water in the tissues to freeze when the surrounding temperature is below 32 degrees Fahrenheit. The primary goal in first aid for frostbite is to prevent additional freezing and further damage to the frozen tissue from thawing and then refreezing. The signs and symptoms are white skin that is waxy and hard to the touch; the area may feel intensely cold and numb; and joint movement may be restricted. In severe frostbite the underlying tissue feels hard.

Give the victim plenty of fluids, rewarm the part only if it is not going to bear weight and will not refreeze, do not rub or massage the area, and evacuate to a hospital.

INSECT BITES AND STINGS

Unless the victim suffers an allergic reaction, bites and stings are usually more painful than serious. For bee stings use a knife edge or fingernail to scrape out the stinger. Do not use tweezers or try to grab the stinger, because you may squeeze more venom into the sting area. Wash the affected area with soap and water and daub on an antisting lotion, Campho Phenique, or a paste of baking soda and water. If the area begins to itch, apply a lotion such as calamine.

If the victim suffers an allergic reaction, give him an antihistamine, keep him calm, maintain the airway, and evacuate to a hospital. People who know that they are allergic will often carry an Ana-Kit, which contains a premeasured injection to fight the reaction.

NOSEBLEED

To treat a nosebleed, remain sitting and apply pressure on the side that is bleeding for at least five minutes. Another suggested method is to pinch the nose just below the bridge and hold for five minutes with the head tilted back. If this does not stop the bleeding, pack the nostril with soft cotton, gauze, or tissue. Sometimes combining this with cold packs on the bridge of the nose will help. Once the bleeding stops, continue resting and do not blow your nose or pick at the encrusted blood. If bleeding does not stop easily, then a visit to the nearest emergency room is recommended.

POISONING

When poisoning is suspected, it is important to seek medical assistance immediately. Find out, if possible, what has caused the poisoning and contact the poison-control center for instructions. In the event that help is not immediately available, there are some steps that can be taken. First, be sure the person is breathing and that he has a pulse. If not, you need to begin CPR. Use caution in giving mouth-to-mouth breathing because it is possible for the rescuer to become poisoned as well—especially if the victim vomits the substance into the rescuer's mouth, which does happen.

In general, you can induce vomiting as long as what was ingested is not a petroleum-based, acid-based, or alkali-based product. In other words, if it has burned on the way down, it will burn on the way up, so do not induce vomiting. Diluting the poison is not an option because it will make the person vomit. For medicine or plant poisoning, dilution and induced vomiting are acceptable.

The best first aid for poisoning is prevention. Teach your children not to eat plants and berries or put things into their mouths. Also be sure all substances are clearly labeled and easily identified. If a fuel bottle containing white gas and a water bottle look similar, you are asking for trouble.

POISON OAK, POISON IVY, AND POISON SUMAC

These plants are regional, so you should inquire which ones grow in your area and learn to identify them. Typically, poison ivy and poison sumac grow in the Midwest and East and poison oak only in the West. Poison oak and poison ivy both go by the rule "leaflets three, let them be." The main differences are that poison oak is a tree or shrub and poison ivy is a vine, and that poison oak leaves are lobed while poison ivy leaves are somewhat jagged. Poison sumac is a shrub that grows mostly in swampy areas and has smooth leaves growing in a single line along each stem and opposite each other. All the plants secrete urushiol, a noxious oil that severely irritates the skin and can be transmitted by direct contact, contact with contaminated clothing or pets, or breathing the smoke.

Signs appear within one to two days after contact. The skin will burn and/or itch, become blistered, and sometimes swell. If the oils have been inhaled, breathing may become very difficult. This is an emergency and will require medical treatment.

If you suspect contact with any one of these poison plants, first remove all contaminated clothing and wash it separately. Second, wash the skin with strong laundry soap or detergent and water. Use warm, not hot, water. Wipe the affected area down with rubbing alcohol.

If a rash develops, avoid scratching because opening the blisters can lead to secondary infection. Contrary to belief, the oozing from a broken blister does not contain urushiol and will not spread the rash. Apply cold compresses and/or a soothing lotion containing hydrocortisone or a similar agent.

SNAKEBITES

The danger from snakebites is greatly blown out of proportion. In the United States there are four poisonous snakes: rattlesnakes, copperheads, coral snakes, and water moccasins, or cottonmouths. These snakes will strike only if aggravated, scared, or surprised with no route of escape. Biting a human is a defensive posture and not an offensive one. Human beings are not and never will be food for a snake! Learn to identify the snakes in your area and the habitat that they most often frequent. In more than twenty years of exploring and hiking all over the United States, Canada, and Baja, Mexico, I have seen fewer than twenty poisonous snakes. Remember that many recorded snakebites have occurred because the snake was being handled.

Snakebite kits are of little use. In most cases, more harm can be done by the first aid performed using a "slice and dice" kit than would have occurred had the victim just been taken to a hospital. If you insist on carrying a snakebite kit, I recommend one that provides powerful suction and does not involve cutting. *Never* apply a tourniquet or ice and never use your mouth to provide suction.

Most experts agree that the recommended first aid for snakebite is as follows: Try to identify the snake so the correct antivenom can be administered quickly. Do not, however, spend time chasing the snake. Do not try to catch or kill it. Clean the wound. Immobilize the injured limb below heart level and keep the victim calm. Apply a pressure bandage directly over the bite area. Get the victim to a hospital as soon as possible.

SPRAINS AND STRAINS

Sprains are caused by a sudden twisting or wrenching of a joint resulting from a hit or fall. The most commonly sprained joints are the wrist, knee, and ankle. It is virtually impossible to distinguish between a break and a sprain without an X-ray, so a first-aider should always assume the limb is broken. Elevate and immobilize the injured limb to relieve pain and prevent further injury. The application of a cold pack is appropriate and will help minimize swelling.

Strains are most often evidenced by sore muscles from overuse. Back, neck, arms, and legs all get a maximum amount of work carrying a backpack—often more than the body is ready for, particularly if you spend most of your time in an office. Children seem less susceptible to strains, although they get them too. An application of gentle heat, massage, and rest should help.

TOOTHACHE

For a simple toothache caused by a cavity, insert a small wad of cotton soaked in oil of cloves into the cavity. This should provide temporary relief.

If the tooth is broken, pack the hole first with cotton soaked in oil of cloves and then with wax to secure the cotton and protect the broken edges.

SUNBURN

Prevention is the best course of action. Sunblock or sunscreen should be applied to all areas of exposed skin. Remember that the higher the elevation, the more intense the sun. Always use a lotion with a sun protection factor (SPF) of fifteen or greater. For younger children and those with very sensitive skin, I recommend twenty-five SPF or greater.

Wear a hat with a wide brim to protect the scalp, face, and neck. Always wear sunglasses, especially in higher altitudes and in snowy conditions. Sunburned (snow-blind) eyes are not only painful, they are dangerous.

If the skin should become burned, keep the burned areas covered with loose clothing. An application of aloe vera gel seems to soothe quite effectively. Do not break blisters if they form because this can lead to infection. Keep the affected area clean.

First Aid and Safety

TICKS

Lyme disease has everyone worried. Although it is only carried by deer ticks, tremendous caution should be taken when traveling in tick country. Ticks are found in woodlands and tall grass, and their legs are designed to grab hold of you as you pass. They are very slow moving but very determined, and they are most active in the spring and summer. Contrary to popular belief, they do not jump on you, nor do they wait high in the branches of a tree to drop down on you, although they will latch on to you as you brush through leaves and branches.

The best first aid is prevention. Always wear light-colored long pants with the legs tucked into your socks and boots. Apply repellent with DEET around all openings such as pant legs, neck, sleeves, waist, and so on. Give everyone a proper tick check and examine the head, neck, back, breasts, and groin. Ticks love warm, snug, and moist areas. If you find a tick embedded in the skin, you should remove it carefully. You will probably need to pull it out using tweezers. Grasp close to the tick's head with the tweezers and pull firmly and steadily, without twisting, until the tick comes out. Check to see that the head has remained attached to its body and is not still embedded in the skin, otherwise a nasty infection could result. Once the tick is removed, cleanse the area thoroughly and then watch to see if a rash develops. Should a rash, headaches, muscle stiffness, or unusual fatigue exhibit itself after a tick bite, let your doctor know because you may need to be treated for Lyme disease. A rash accompanied by a fever may indicate another tick-induced disease, Rocky Mountain spotted fever. Seek medical assistance immediately.

MEDICINES AND DRUGS

Pain-Relief Drugs and Topical Applications *Do not administer any of these drugs to a child without the express guidance and direction of a medical doctor.*

Aspirin: Mild analgesic, anti-inflammatory, fever reduction. Interferes with blood clotting, can cause nausea, don't give to children.

Motrin: Anti-inflammatory and moderate pain relief. May cause stomach irritation and nausea.

Tylenol: For relief of minor to moderate pain such as muscle ache and inflammation. May cause liver damage if overdosed. This drug is used as primary pain relief in many first-aid kits.

Wilderness with Children

Tylenol with codeine (narcotic, prescription only): For pain and reduction of fever. Codeine sometimes causes nausea, constipation, and allergic reactions.

Lidocaine Gel 2 Percent (prescription only): Topical pain relief/local anesthetic.

Allergic Reaction Drugs and Topical Applications

Benadryl: Acts as an antihistamine, sedative, and anti-itch treatment. Use with caution; may cause drowsiness, constipation, weakness, headache, difficulty in urination, diarrhea.

Ana-Kit: Injection of epinephrine and Chlo-Amine tablets to relieve severe allergic reaction. May cause headache, anxiety, heart palpitations.

Caladryl lotion: A calamine and Benadryl lotion to relieve minor skin irritations.

Hydrocortisone Ointment 25 Percent: Steroid ointment for more severe skin reactions.

Gastrointestinal

Lomotil: To control diarrhea. Use only if the diarrhea compromises safety or an ability to travel, because it is possible to introduce serious infection and start a fever because of bowel retention.

Maalox: Neutralizes stomach acids and relieves indigestion. Can produce mild diarrhea.

Antibiotic Drugs and Ointments *You must know what infection you are treating, otherwise the antibiotic is worthless. Broad-spectrum antibiotics are best, but you should always be aware of what specific type of infections will most likely be encountered.*

Septra DS (prescription only): Treats urinary tract infections and diarrhea. May cause allergic reaction.

Keflex (prescription only): Fights skin infections and respiratory, urinary, and inner ear infections. May cause allergic reaction.

Neosporin Ointment: Helps prevent infection in minor cuts and abrasions.

Antiseptic

Betadine: Use for topical cleaning of skin around the wound or before lancing a blister. If using to clean a wound, use 25 percent Betadine to 75 percent sterile water. Never use Betadine in a deep wound.

Skin Preparation

Tincture of Benzoin: Prepares skin for application of adhesive.

Other Drugs to Consider

Cough suppressant: For example, Robitussin with codeine.

Decongestant: For example, Afrin Nasal Spray (not recommended for prolonged periods or for use at high altitudes), Sudafed, Actifed.

Antibiotic Eye Drops: For example, Neosporin Opthalmic Drops.

Skin Care: For example, A and D Ointment, which soothes rashes and dry skin.

Bandages, Dressings, and Other Items

Sterile gauze pads in a variety of two-by-two and four-by-four-inch pads

Roller gauze: Kling or Kerlex

Nonadhering dressing: Telfa pads (coat with antibacterial ointment or petroleum, but change frequently to prevent drying out and adhering to the skin)

One-inch adhesive tape

Butterfly bandages or Steristrips assortment

Ace Wrap: Three-inch-wide bandage

Large compress: Use feminine hygiene pads

Assortment of cloth Band-Aids (I also recommend carrying some Snoopy Strips—children seem to love them)

Moleskin (for the prevention and treatment of friction and blisters)

SecondSkin (When the blister forms, it will provide soothing protection in most instances, although I have known it to stick to the wound and create a painful and difficult removal.)

Triangular bandage (for holding dressings in place, attaching splints, and creating slings)

Equipment and Accessories

Tweezers

Needle

Single-sided razor blade

Bandage scissors

Irrigation syringe

Low-reading thermometer

SAM Splint or wire mesh

Space blanket
Waterproof matches
Emergency report form
Pencil
Emergency phone numbers and money for a phone call
Snakebite kit: compress, suction (use a Sawyer Kit)
Dental kit: oil of cloves, cotton pads, wax

TIPS IN A NUTSHELL

1. Teach caution when your children are playing on rocks, rubble, brush piles, and fallen logs.

2. Teach them to be wary of snow, ice, riverbanks, mud, and poisonous plants.

3. Help your children to respect but not be afraid of animals. Most animals, including snakes, will not bite unless badgered, teased, or threatened in some manner.

4. Learn CPR and basic first-aid skills. Be sure your children learn these skills as well.

5. Practice first-aid and emergency situations before going on a hike or trip.

CHAPTER 10

Survival and Emergencies

F EAR AND PANIC ARE BY far the greatest dangers to any person in the wilderness. While it is true that natural acts and other unforeseen circumstances claim injuries and lives each year, most deaths and injuries can be prevented by staying calm and thinking through the situation. Staying calm is not easy to do, however, especially if you have only limited knowledge or information upon which to base your decisions. This is why it is so important to teach your children basic wilderness skills that will help them in an emergency. Teach them how to stay found, how to build a fire, how to look for shelter, where to find water, and other basic survival skills.

This is not going to be a dissertation on survival skills for children. There are already a number of good books on the market that provide such information. This chapter will help you give the bare essentials of information to your children, so that they will feel comfortable and safe—even in stressful situations.

THE ART OF STAYING FOUND

It has been said of Daniel Boone that when asked if he was ever lost, his reply was, "Disoriented for a couple of days, maybe. Lost, never." The major difference between Boone and the majority of weekend wilderness explorers is one of skill. Boone could always hunt, trap, find water, build a shelter, make a boat, and gradually find his way out of a predicament. The average family, however, has neither the skills to survive off the land nor the time to spend wandering aimlessly.

It is important for parents to realize that anyone can get lost. All it takes is a dense mist, a few unplanned turns in the woods, nightfall, or a storm to disorient most people. The so-called instinctive sense of direction is only as good as the information provided to create that sense. I have seen people who swore up and down that they had an infallible sense of direction get utterly lost after I led them on a short, albeit circuitous, hike away from camp.

A good sense of direction comes from keeping your senses wide open to all sources of information: sights, sounds, smells, and even feel. Teach your children to be aware of significant landmarks such as a tall tree, a prominent rock, a large meadow. Teach them also to look in 360-degree sweeps. They should look at the route you are traveling from the front, side, and back. Quite often a tree that looked unique in one direction looks completely different when viewed from another.

Sounds such as a river, cars on a road, and a foghorn on a lighthouse are also important bits of information. Don't overlook the smell and feel of an area. A valley may feel damp and smell a certain way. Water can quite often be smelled from a distance. Individually, each of the senses contains a fragment of information to help you and your children stay oriented. Combine all the fragments into careful and complete observation and you begin to create a "good sense of direction."

Many of us have heard it hundreds of times, but I am going to say it again: "Plan your hike and hike your plan." Good planning goes far in ensuring a safe trip. Teach your children about the area you are visiting, too. Most children will find topo maps confusing and impossible to understand. Try, instead, to draw a special map for your children. Show them major landmarks, where the roads are, how the trail looks, where the water sources are, where you plan to camp, and the location of some of the nearby towns.

A child should never leave camp alone, under any circumstances. In addition, no one should ever leave home or camp without telling someone responsible where he is going. This applies to adults and children. There are no exceptions to these rules, and they must become a hard-and-fast law for your family.

Younger children have a habit of wandering off without realizing the direction in which they are headed. It can seem that getting sidetracked is a young child's mission in life. Often wandering from one adventure to another without care, a child can suddenly look around to discover that nothing looks familiar. Because of this, you will have to watch your children extremely closely. I recommend that each child in your family knows his home address, phone number, parents' names, and campsite number, if applicable. If the child has trouble remembering all this, write it down and have him carry it in a safe place or wear it like a name tag.

Children of all ages should carry a whistle. The sound of a whistle is much more easily heard and more energy efficient than a tiny voice screaming for help. Teach your children to blow the whistle loudly and distinctly in sets of three: *tweet - tweet - tweet*. This is a universal signal for help, and help will arrive if anyone is within earshot. Although blowing on the whistle is very attractive to children, you must teach them to use it only in an emergency.

Children should gradually and very patiently be taught visual navigation without the aid of a map. In other words, how to get from point A to point B, and then be able to return to A. This is done by continually observing and remembering prominent landmarks or features of the terrain they are traveling through. You must encourage them to take time to make a mental map so that this becomes an unconscious habit. As children grow older and show an aptitude for and interest in map reading, then add that to their arsenal of wilderness skills.

The way to teach children to observe distant and nearby landmarks and features is to frequently stop and have them pick out features that they will remember. At each subsequent stop, have your children recite each landmark they have selected up until this point. Your children should be looking for features such as distant peaks, far-off ridges, a towering grove of trees that stands separate and above the rest, the distinct shape of a meadow, a strangely shaped tree or bush, a cave, a stream, and so on. Once you reach the point of turning around and heading back, take time to sit down with your children and challenge them to remember what it is they will be looking for along the way. Help them remember the landmarks if necessary. Then put your children in charge as they navigate from recognizable landmark to recognizable landmark all the way back to home or camp.

Remember to be very patient and loving. Initially, and especially if they are very young, children are apt to forget things and get somewhat distracted.

WHAT LOST CHILDREN SHOULD DO

"I'm lost!" That initial moment of panic surges through the human mind and body like a runaway train. If not controlled, the body soon follows the urge to act like such a train and takes off plowing through bushes, trees, meadows in a desperate effort to be found. This type of panic is all too common and can lead to complete exhaustion, dehydration, injury, and even death.

Your children must be taught to sit down and think quietly if they are lost. It is when children panic and begin to frantically try to find their way to home or camp that they usually get in deeper trouble. If your children will sit down and think, a solution will usually become evident. Teach them to look around painstakingly, retracing their steps in their mind. Very often, after some calm thinking, the trail or route home usually can be discovered.

Sometimes, however, the route home is not clearly evident, so your child may feel a need to get up and explore the surrounding area in search of a trail. This is okay if the child can mark the area where he or she is now standing and be able to return to it after the initial search. From that original point, the child can begin working his way outward in a circular pattern until a familiar piece of ground or terrain is discovered. While working their way out in this fashion, it is important for your children to always keep their starting position in sight.

From each familiar point that is discovered, your children should be taught to find another landmark that now identifies this area. Essentially, they are moving from familiar point to familiar point and marking their progress along the way. Once the children discover a trail or road that is recognizable, they can then head out in a straight line toward home or help.

It is equally critical for your children to understand the importance of staying in one place if they have no idea where they are. Wandering children make for extremely difficult rescues.

I feel somewhat strange mentioning molestation in this context, but it is an important consideration. In this day and age, children are molested and

Survival and Emergencies   97

come to harm, often when they are perceived to be the most helpless. It is vitally important that you teach your children not to thankfully run into the arms of a waiting stranger who seems to be offering help. Give your children some idea of who to trust and who should be treated with caution so they can make that decision for themselves should the need arise. My daughter has been taught to trust a police officer, a ranger, and adults in groups. Individual men who are offering help are immediately suspect. It sickens me to have to teach her not to trust, but with the rate of abductions and molestations on the rise, I have no choice.

FINDING SHELTER

If a child is lost and has no idea where home or camp lies, then finding shelter is the first survival skill to master. Although there are usually small caves, deadfalls, hollow logs, and eroded overhangs that appear to be good shelters in warm and sunny weather, these natural shelters are often not ideal. At best, natural enclosures can provide only temporary refuge and, at worst, can become death traps.

The criteria governing the selection of adequate shelter are wind protection, heat retention, and rain or snow protection. Wind protection is extremely important because a strong wind coupled with rain will rob the body of heat and can cause extreme hypothermia, even when the air temperature is 50 degrees. Wind also rapidly increases the rate of dehydration. Wind protection is the easiest to find because almost anything—a fallen log, a dense bush, or a large rock—will break the wind.

Rain or snow protection is more difficult to locate because the shelter must provide protection from above as well as from the sides. Dense bushes, thick brush piles, downed trees, natural caves, and large rock piles are all candidates for a natural shelter that will protect from wind and rain.

Most natural shelters cannot provide the third important criteria for shelter selection—heat retention. If you and your children study the way animals construct their burrows or nests, you will find that they hollow out an area in a tree or the ground, then line or stuff it with leaves, grasses, twigs, and even fur. Children should be taught to gather dead leaves, twigs, and grasses to line and stuff the shelter they select to help them stay warm.

Natural shelters can be dangerous and your children must be taught to identify the dangers. For example, deadfalls, rock piles, and caves are all

Wilderness with Children

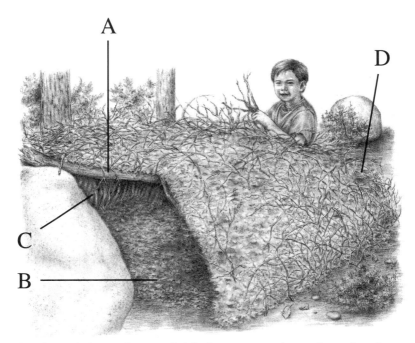

The above shelter is shown unfinished so you can picture the various layers. A—Support pole. B—Leaves, which should fill inside completely. C—Inside framework of sticks. D—Alternating layers of leaves and twigs for insulation and protection.

potential homes to a variety of animals and insects. Care must be taken not to suddenly disturb a nest of bees, a poisonous snake, bears, and so on. Perhaps even more dangerous is the possibility that the natural shelter could collapse at any moment and trap the child. Children should also be very cautious around deadfalls. Where one tree has fallen, more may be ready to tumble.

Another possible hazard to a natural shelter is that it camouflages whatever is in it very well. When I was actively involved in search-and-rescue missions, I was on one particular rescue where we were looking for an older man who had been missing for several days. It had snowed heavily, covering all previous signs and making it difficult for the dogs to find any scent. All we had to go on was instinct and educated guesses based on the lay of the land and our deductions as to how this individual would have traveled.

We swept the area for several days, back and forth, covering every inch with what we thought was a fine-toothed comb. We found no sign of the man and were forced to give up. Later that month, after all the snow had melted, a man hiking in that area stumbled across the victim's pack near a downed tree. Looking farther, he found the man huddled inside the trunk with branches pulled in front of the opening to protect him from the snow. The man had frozen to death, and we had walked back and forth in front of that tree on several occasions without realizing he was in there.

As a consequence of that search, I recommend that anyone who uses a natural shelter should leave some sign outside the shelter that he or she is inside. The sign should be obvious and visible so it will not be obscured by snow or debris falling on the ground.

Building a shelter is the best way for your child to provide himself with warmth, security, and dryness, and a constructed shelter does stand out from the surrounding environment. While many survival books teach you to build lean-tos, A-frames, igloos, and even cabins, the quickest and most efficient shelter to create is one I was taught to build at camp. It uses only material lying on the forest floor and requires no tools to build. A child can construct this shelter in about one and a half hours. To build the shelter, pick an area that has good drainage, is not going to get washed away, and will not be buried by a falling tree or rock avalanche. Also make certain that the area you have selected is not over an animal hole, an ant's nest, or a thicket of poison oak, poison ivy, or poison sumac.

At the shelter site find a large rock, stump, log, or other support. I was taught to use a log or downed tree as one wall, but a downed tree with an adequate trunk is not always present. Ideally, the log or rock support should be about three feet high. Find a large stick several inches across and approximately five feet long—or longer if the person using it is taller. Lean one end of the stick on the rock, log, or stump so the other end rests on the ground forming a diagonal ridgepole for your shelter. Collect a large number of smaller sticks to lean along each side of the ridgepole and create a frame for your shelter. Remember to leave an opening or door by the boulder, stump, or log and to one side, away from the wind. Now have your child crawl inside the shelter to make sure there is enough room to comfortably lie down, so that he does not kick or disturb the sides when moving around inside.

Next, pile twigs, lots of dried leaves, and small branches on top of the framework. This should be a generous layer—approximately two- to three-feet thick is appropriate. The final tier should be a snug layer of small branches and twigs, heavy enough to help hold the inner layer in place, even in a strong wind, but not so heavy that it crushes or compresses the leaves and twigs making up the inner lining. Finally, stuff the inside of the shelter full of dried leaves, pine needles, ferns, and so on, so the interior is loosely filled from top to bottom. With the shelter now complete, all your child has to do is squirm and snuggle feet-first inside. This type of shelter will keep a child or adult warm and dry for days, even in the worst conditions.

FINDING WATER

Water is second only to finding shelter in the scale of importance for survival situations. Dehydration is a killer. Your children should know that with a good shelter and a supply of water, a person can survive for a very long time, even with no food. Your children should also be wary of water, because most water on the earth is polluted to some degree. Chemically or biologically, these pollutants can turn a very basic survival situation into a critical emergency. For this reason water must be treated or purified to be considered safe.

Water can be found or created. The easiest way to get water is to discover a stream or moving water source. Moving water is the least likely to be polluted. Tree stumps, potholes, and stagnant ponds are other water sources, although these are the most likely to be dangerously tainted. Sometimes digging a hole into a damp streambed will uncover a water source that can fill the hole. Water can even be obtained from dew-soaked leaves and grasses. Instead of crawling around licking the leaves, soak up the moisture with a cotton cloth and then wring the water into your mouth.

There are several ways to treat water. The boiling method is the best guarantee of purification. If your child has a pot or cup, he or she can build a fire and boil the water for five to six minutes to purify it. Boiling will destroy all biological pollutants.

Filtering will not remove the most dangerous pollutants because in a survival situation most children will not be carrying a commercial filter with them. To filter very muddy or debris-filled water, pour the water through a bandana or other piece of cotton clothing so particles are removed.

Chemical purification works very well in removing biological, but not chemical, impurities. Products made of iodine, such as Potable Aqua or Polar Pure, are easy to use and very effective water treatments. Teach your child how to use these properly and safely. If your child carries a compact survival kit, include a bottle of Potable Aqua.

Water distilled by a solar still is a method of creating pure water where there is none evident. It requires a large piece of plastic, a cup, and a length of plastic tubing. Find an area that is damp, in a dry streambed, or at the bottom of a gully, and dig a hole about two feet deep and three feet wide. Place a cup in the center of the hole and put one end of the plastic tubing in the bottom of the cup. The earth you are digging should be damp near the bottom. If it is dry, drop in green leaves, urinate in it, or add a small amount of water to provide moisture for condensation. Cover the hole with the clear plastic sheet and leave the other end of the plastic tube protruding to one side. Seal the edges with dirt so no moisture can escape and no air can enter. Finally, weigh down the center of the sheet with a rock, so that the point of the inverted cone is directly above the cup.

The sun, even on a hazy or partly cloudy day, will warm the earth and cause moisture from the soil to evaporate, condensing on the underside of the plastic. The condensation will roll down the sheet and drop into the cup. You will be able to drink out of the cup by using the accessible end of the plastic tube. This method works well and the condensation or distilled water is pure, even if the moisture source is not.

When you teach your children about water, you have an excellent opportunity to bring home an environmental lesson—the impact of pollution. As you tell them about the importance of water, and that they must always treat it, explain that until very recently most water was pure. Not so long ago humans could drink directly from many streams and rivers, but now, with garbage, human and animal waste, and chemicals entering our water sources, every drop of water on the earth is becoming seriously polluted. Perhaps this will get them to think twice about their impact on the earth.

BUILDING FIRES

Fire building is an important skill, yet it is not as essential as building a shelter or finding water; you can stay warm without a fire. Still, it is valuable and, in many instances, necessary for water purification, additional warmth, cooking, and even signaling.

What is most important to teach children about fire is to respect it. While it is a source of warmth and heat for cooking, it is also a very dangerous tool, capable of destroying vast amounts of land and many animals if it burns out of control. Not all children should be allowed to build fires, and there is no hard-and-fast rule about what age is appropriate. I was building fires from scratch at age eight, and yet I had several friends who should not have been trusted with a match until age eighteen—even then there was some question.

The teaching process begins with helping to collect wood and with careful observation of a parent building and maintaining the fire. Children will soon learn where to find the driest wood on the ground, how to find dry kindling under logs or around the base of a pine tree, what type and shape of wood is best used for kindling, and what is best for feeding the fire. They will also learn, in very wet conditions when a fire is necessary for survival, to overlook the rule of not breaking dead branches and twigs off trees. Teach your children to avoid poison oak, poison ivy, and poison sumac—inhaling the smoke from any of these poisonous plants is very irritating to the skin, eyes, and lungs, and often dangerous.

As your children become proficient at collecting and gathering suitable wood, they can begin helping to maintain the fire. When maintaining the fire, they will learn how to create proper coals for cooking, how to keep the flames from getting too hot, how to safely feed the flames with wood, and how best to put out a fire.

Once children have responsibly gathered wood and maintained the flame, it is time to learn how to build the fire. It is appropriate to bestow some award upon the child when reaching this honored position; it helps give him a feeling of the importance of this task. Lord of the Fire Builders and Honored Member of the Fire Clan are two of my favorites.

Teach your child to select a fire area that is free from ground debris, roots, and other vegetation, which might catch fire and spread the flames to surrounding trees. The fire should also not be built under overhanging tree

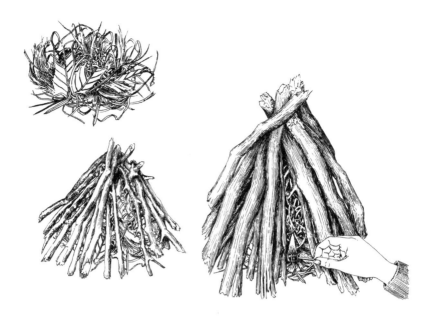

A tepee fire is perhaps the easiest and most efficient of all fires to build. Create a ball of kindling or dried grasses, frayed bark, and tiny twigs. Add a layer of small sticks. Add a final layer of sticks no thicker than two fingers and ignite.

limbs or within ten to fifteen feet of any shelter. Building a fire in a cave or next to wet or damp rocks is dangerous, too, because water or moisture in the rocks can be brought to the boiling point and the resulting steam will expand and explode the rock, much like a bomb. When I was ten, a member of our campfire group tossed a wet sandstone rock into the fire. It exploded and sent embers showering over all of us. Fortunately no one was hurt, but the potential for serious injury was very high.

Show children how to pick an area that has natural wind breaks and how to clear the area of all loose debris. Once the area is clear of debris, teach them to dig into the dirt to create a shallow depression approximately six to twelve inches deep and two to two and a half feet across. Ring the depression with rocks to help contain the fire. Finally, create a heat reflector and wind break on the windward side of the ring. The break should be a half-

Wilderness with Children

circle shape and provide an adequate shield against the wind and a surface to reflect the heat toward the person sitting by the fire.

Once the fire site has been safely prepared, the child needs to gather plenty of kindling and enough wood to comfortably last the night. Beginning with the kindling, bunch up a ball of frayed bark, dried grasses, and tiny twigs from a pine tree, evergreen, or other available tree. Now, lay very small twigs and sticks, not much larger than the kindling, up against one another and over the ball to form a cone or tepee shape. Leave a small opening through which you can place the match to ignite the fire. Continue adding more wood, gradually longer and thicker, up to the width of two fingers. Maintain the cone shape at all times. When the fire is built to satisfaction, a match is carefully struck, shielded from the wind, and placed next to the waiting kindling to ignite it.

This fire is the most easily constructed and is quickly lit, even in severe weather. It will put out a tremendous amount of heat, even with a relatively small flame, and it is quite easy to maintain. When adding wood, lay each piece carefully into the flame and always keep the cone shape intact. Instruct your children not to toss or arbitrarily throw wood on a fire; at best, this sends up a shower of sparks and, at worst, they could destroy the fire.

SURVIVAL TESTS

One of the best ways to teach your children to survive in the wilderness is to simulate survival situations during camping trips. I remember when I learned to make a shelter, build a fire, and "live off the land"; there was an air of adventure in it. We were learning about Indian lore—reading their stories, dancing their dances, studying animals, and using our imaginations to the maximum. We even became a special clan and lived in the woods for a while. It was in this atmosphere of mystery and adventure that we made our fires, built our shelters, and searched for water. Sure, we weren't becoming hardened survivalists (we were given three waterproof matches with which to build a fire and camp was one mile from home), but we were taught to use our heads, not panic, and feel comfortable in the outdoors.

Your children will learn much about the land, and themselves, if an air of mystery and adventure is created for them. Become explorers for a weekend, form your own Indian clan, or pretend to be hibernating bears— anything to create a mood of fun and learning. Take all your camping gear with you to a local park, campground, or even your own backyard, but don't use your tent, stove, or sleeping bag unless necessary. Build your own shelters and sleep in them, make a fire and cook with it, and make water and drink it. Most of all, have fun and listen to your children learn and teach.

TIPS IN A NUTSHELL

1. Teach children to keep their eyes moving in 360-degree sweeps as they walk. Tell them to remember important and easy to recognize landmarks to use in finding their way later. Children should use their eyes, ears, and nose in helping determine the location of camp.

2. No one should ever leave camp alone.

3. Instead of trying to teach small children to read a topographical map, create special hand-drawn maps for them that feature major landmarks, roads, trails, water sources, camp, and nearby towns. Show them how to use the map.

4. Instruct your children how and when to use the whistle around their necks. (Three distinct whistle blasts indicate trouble.)

5. Teach your children to sit and think quietly if they become disoriented. Panic will only get them more lost. If they clearly remember the way back to camp, they should proceed as long as everything continues to look familiar. Otherwise, they must stay put.

6. If lost, step number one is to find or build a shelter. A shelter made of sticks and debris is very effective and quite warm.

7. Finding water is the second step. Show your child how to make or hunt for water.

8. Making a fire is third priority. Fires are important for warmth and for signaling.

9. Last on the list is finding food. Teach your child not to eat plants unless they are certain they are not poisonous. With shelter and water a child can survive for a long time without getting into trouble, even if no food is available.

Family Adventure Checklist

The following checklist will help plan your next family adventure. Not all the items included will be needed on every trip. Pack only what you need and leave the rest at home; remember, you've got to carry what you pack.

PACKS
    Backpack (external or internal frame)
    Waterproof pack cover
    Child carrier
    Day pack or fanny pack

SHELTER
    Lightweight tent (including poles, stakes, and guy lines)
    Mosquito netting (for around head when sleeping under the stars)
    Nine-foot by twelve-foot nylon tarp with grommets

SLEEPING
    Sleeping bag (down or synthetic)
    Sleeping pad
    Pillow
    Ground cloth

TEN-PLUS ESSENTIALS
    Sunglasses
    Water bottle

Nylon cord (50 feet)
Waterproof/windproof matches
Flashlight (extra bulb and batteries)
Fire starter
Pocket knife
Toilet paper
Topographic map
Compass
Emergency blanket
Whistle
Signal mirror
Emergency snacks

KITCHEN
Stove
Fuel/fuel bottle
Primer paste
Lighter or matches
Windscreen
Cook set
Frying pan
Water bag (collapsible)
Storage containers for food
Ziploc bags (freezer variety)
Large spoon
Knife
Spatula
Can opener (GI folding variety)
Small whisk
Small grater
Pot grips
Knife, fork, spoon
Plate
Cup
Bowl
Cutting board (small nylon variety)

Ice chest
Scrub pads
Biodegradable soap
Paper towels
Aluminum foil
Spice kit

FIRST-AID KIT
(See chapter 9)

TOILETRIES
Comb, brush
Toothbrush, toothpaste
Dental floss
Deodorant
Small towel
Shaving kit
Biodegradable skin and hair soap
Moisturizing lotion
Towlettes
Sunscreen (15 SPF or better)
Lip balm
Tampons

CLOTHING
First Layer:
Underwear
Long underwear (tops and bottoms)
Liner socks
Wool outer socks
T-shirt
Second Layer:
Wool shirt
Synchilla or wool sweater
Shorts
Long pants

Protective Layer:
Wool or Synchilla hat
Sun hat
Bunting or Synchilla jacket
Parka (synthetic or down)
Wool mittens
Rain suit (jacket and pants)
Gaitors
Windbreaker
Hiking boots
Camp shoes or sneakers

MISCELLANEOUS GEAR
Butane or candle lantern
Fishing gear and fishing license
Trowel
Thermometer
Bandana
Note pad and pencil
Camera, film, lenses
Binoculars
Plastic trash bags

FUN AND GAMES
Frisbee
Nerf ball
Hacky Sack
Cards
Miniature games (backgammon, checkers, chess, and so on)
Harmonica
Kazoo
Paperback books
Coloring books
Star guide
Mini microscope
Magnifying glass

Wilderness with Children

Small plastic collection containers
Aquarium net
Sketch pad
Pencils
Crayons
Colored felt-tip pens
Gold pan and mineral book

BICYCLE TOURING AND MOUNTAIN BIKING
Cycling shorts
Cycling gloves
Cycling shoes
Helmet
Tire-patch kit
Spare parts
Mini tool kit

CROSS-COUNTRY SKIING
Waxless skis
Boots
Bindings
Poles
Extra ski tip
Basic repair parts

CANOEING
Canoe
Paddles
Life jackets
Waterproof duffle bags
Waterproof containers for camera gear
Rope to secure duffles and contents in boat

SPECIAL CONSIDERATIONS FOR INFANTS
Bottles and extra nipples
Rubber or plastic pants

Diapers
Sleep suits
Extra clothing
Warm snuggle suit
Rain suit
Baby food
Baby wipes
Baby powder or corn starch

Surviving the Car Trip

Sanely reaching your chosen destination with a car full of gear and playful children can often be a challenging adventure in itself. I have heard from many parents, and I must confess I am one too, who have occasionally considered murder as an acceptable alternative to control a boisterous carload of children. While there is never any guarantee of a smooth and enjoyable journey, there are some methods that will minimize those dreaded trips to hell.

The following are suggested items to pack and/or tips to consider that will help make your next car trip more pleasurable for everyone—including the children.

FIRM TRAVEL RULES

No screaming, loud noises, or strange sounds that irritate.

Keep the back seat clean—no more than one activity or toy out at any one time.

CHILDREN'S TRAVEL ACTIVITY BAG

Purpose: To provide quiet entertainment to pass the time in car or restaurant.

Contents: Plain and lined paper, clipboard (a portable desk), markers (crayons melt when left in a hot car), small plastic toys (cars, animals, and so on), a multitude of stickers, envelopes, safety scissors, Scotch tape, activity and coloring books, and picture and reading books.

Special tips: Pack all the items in a day pack or very small duffle bag.

Items in the bag should be used only on car trips and not played with at any other time. The quickest way to make the contents of the bag unappealing is to allow your children to play with them at home.

Your children should be the ones who determine what goes in the bag, and they should know that they get to play with the contents only during car trips.

PARENTS' MAGIC BAG

Purpose: To provide additional games, activities, and distractions to keep everyone in the car happy and cooperative.

Contents: Card games (Snap, Go Fish, and so on), small magnetic games (checkers, chess, Chinese checkers), surprise activity book, special surprise gift (small and wrapped—toys, books, and so on), favorite stuffed animal.

Special Tips: Don't let your children see what is in the bag—everything must be a surprise for maximum benefit.

MUNCHIES AND CLEANUP BOX

Purpose: To provide healthy and delicious snacks for the road while preventing the car and children from becoming a sticky mess.

Contents: Favorite snacks (raisins, nuts, crackers, cheese cubes, dried fruit), favorite fruits and beverages, Wet Ones, paper towels, straws (which make beverages easier and neater to drink in a moving car), freezer-size Ziploc bags (for packing trash—bag top prevents food and liquid from spilling).

Special Tips: Children may enjoy packing their own lunch boxes—as they would for school. Be sure to supervise and not allow too much candy or messy food. Don't pack too much. It is easier to stop for a soda than to deal with the leftovers that have been "sun-ripened." For children who are prone to spilling, use ice water as a beverage. It won't stain if dumped on the seat.

COMFORT TIPS

Include pillows and blankets for everyone; even a two-hour ride will seem much longer if tired children cannot get comfortable—especially on the ride home. Have a box of Kleenex for runny noses and simple cleanups. Wear comfortable clothes for the ride. Sweats are my recommendation. It

Wilderness with Children

is no fun to ride home in sweaty or very dirty clothes, so have a clean set available.

Use a roof-top carrier for packs, duffles, and extra gear that will not fit in the trunk. The more space available inside the car, the less stress everyone will feel and the lower the chances of tempers boiling over.

SILENCE TIP

For unusually boisterous children, I have heard the following works quite well. Give each child an equal roll of quarters, Life Savers, and so on at the start of each trip. They are not allowed to eat or use the roll until the car trip is over. Explain to them that each time they are told to be quiet, they will have to give up one quarter or Life Saver. Whatever they have leftover after the trip is theirs to keep—if they go into debt, they will receive less the next time. Sure, this could be called bribery or buying good behavior, but in a cramped car, if it works, it works!

CAR GAMES

The following is a sample list of some of my favorite car games. These games are ideal when other quiet activities no longer work and everyone needs something to take his mind off the road, the cramped car, and how long it is going to take to get there. Many of these are also excellent trail and campfire games.

Only twice have I found that car games were not appropriate: when everyone was already quietly entertaining themselves; and when the driver was heavily concentrating during very bad weather or extremely heavy traffic.

I Spy: Player One selects an item and gives a color or shape clue. (The item should be in the car or visible for at least several minutes. Outside items that whiz by are difficult to guess and even more difficult to prove that they were selected.) Everyone guesses. Player One continues to give clues until the object is guessed. If everyone is stumped, then Player One gets another turn.

What Am I? Player One chooses a category, such as food, useful object, natural object, plant, animal, and so on. Player One then gives several clues in the form of a sentence: "I am a plant; I grow in fields and have a tall stalk." Everyone gets one guess. Give another clue if necessary: "I have ears." Everyone gets another guess. If they can't guess after four clues, then Player One goes again. (The answer, by the way, is corn.)

Name That Tune: One player sings or hums a song and the others have to name the song, or the movie or TV show that it comes from.

Sing-along: Children love to sing, but for your own sanity, stay away from "Ninety-nine bottles of soda on the wall." Some children have the uncanny endurance to be able to sing it to completion and then, yep, you guessed it, one more time around.

Don't Finish That Word: Player One thinks of a word and then says the first letter of the word aloud, such as B for the word "become." Each player then adds a letter, each with his or her own word in mind, such as A for "baby." The object is not to be the player who completes the word. Every time a player completes a word, he or she is given a point. The player with the least number of points at the end of the game wins. Hint: The strategy is to try to get other players to spell and complete a word that must end on anyone's turn but your own.

Fantasy Time: Every person must respond to hypothetical questions such as these: If you could go anywhere in the world, where would you go and why? If you could be any animal or bird, what would you be and why? If you could be another person for a day, who would you be and why? If you found a bottle with a magic genie living in it who would grant you three wishes, what would you wish for and why? If a visitor from outer space landed in your yard and asked you to describe your country, how would you do it?

Recommended Reading

MAGAZINES

Backpacker, 33 East Minor St., Emmaus, PA 18098
Bicycling, 33 East Minor St., Emmaus, PA 18098
Canoe, P.O. Box 3146, Kirkland, WA 98083
Outside, 1165 North Clark St., Chicago, IL 60610

BOOKS

Axcell, Claudia, Diana Cooke, and Vikki Kinmont. *Simple Foods for the Pack*. San Francisco: Sierra Club Books, 1986.

Barker, Harriett. *Supermarket Backpacker*. New York: Contemporary Books, 1977.

Bowden, Marcia. *Nature for the Very Young*. New York: John Wiley & Sons, Inc., 1986.

Brown, Tom. *Tom Brown's Field Guide to Nature and Survival for Children*. New York: Berkeley Publishing Group, 1989.

Chambers, Patricia. *River Runners' Recipes*. Seattle: Pacific Search Press, 1984.

Cornell, Joseph. *Sharing Nature with Children*. Nevada City, CA: Dawn Publications, 1979.

Fletcher, Colin. *The New Complete Walker III*. New York: Alfred A. Knopf, 1986.

Gillette, Ned, and John Dostal. *Cross-Country Skiing*. Seattle: The Mountaineers, 1988.

Harrison, David, and Judy Harrison. *Canoe Tripping with Children*. Merrillville, IN: ICS Books, Inc., 1990.

Mooers, Robert L., Jr. *Finding Your Way in the Outdoors*. Danbury, CT: Outdoor Life Books, 1972.

The Mountaineers. *Mountaineering First Aid*. Seattle: The Mountaineers, 1985.

Shepardson, Carl. *The Family Canoe Trip*. Merrillville, IN: ICS Books, Inc., 1985.

Simer, Peter, and John Sullivan. *The National Outdoor Leadership School's Wilderness Guide*. New York: Simon and Schuster, 1983.

Equipment Suppliers

MAIL-ORDER CAMPING EQUIPMENT COMPANIES

Bike Nashbar, 4111 Simon Road, Youngstown, OH 44512 (800-627-4227)

Campmor, 810 Rt. 17 N., Paramus, NJ 07653 (800-526-4784)

L. L. Bean, Inc., Casco St., Freeport, ME 04033 (800-221-4221)

The Nature Company, P.O. Box 2310, Berkeley, CA 94702 (800-227-1114)

Recreational Equipment, Inc., P.O. Box 88125-BL, Seattle, WA 98138 (800-426-4840)

Northwest River Supplies, P.O. Box 9186OS, Moscow, ID 83843 (800-635-5202)

Don Gleason's Campers Supply, Inc., 439 Pearl St., Northampton, MA 01061 (413-584-4895)

NAME-BRAND EQUIPMENT AND CLOTHING FOR CHILDREN

Alpenlite, 3891 Ventura Ave., Ventura, CA 93001 (805-653-0431): day packs and smaller soft packs

American Widgeon, 376 Brannan St., San Francisco, CA 94107 (415-974-6803): clothing

The Baby Bag Co., P.O. Box 566, Cumberland Center, ME 04021 (207-829-5038): specialized sleeping bags and sleep sacks of fiberfill and bunting

Bell Helmets, 15301 Shoemaker Ave., P.O. Box 1020, Norwalk, CA 90680 (800-486-BELL): bicycle helmets

Bolder Designs, 1580 Canyon Blvd., Boulder, CO 80302 (303-443-1925): custom-designed sleeping bags

Burley Design Cooperative, 4080 Stewart Rd., Dept. F, Eugene, OR 97402 (503-687-1644): bicycle trailers

Campmor, 810 Rt. 17 N., Paramus, NJ 07653 (800-526-4784): clothing

Camp Trails, P.O. Box 966, Binghamton, NY 13902 (607-779-2200): day packs and small frame packs

Cannondale, 9 Brookside Pl., Georgetown, CT 06829 (203-838-4488): bicycle trailers

Caribou Mountaineering, P.O. Box 3696, Chico, CA 95927 (800-824-4153): day packs and sleeping bags

Cherry Tree Co., Inc., 166 Valley St., Providence, RI 02909 (401-421-8911): clothing

Chuck Roast, Odell Hill Rd., Conway, NH 03818 (603-447-5492): clothing

Coleman Company, 250 N. St. Francis, Wichita, KS 67201 (316-261-3485): day packs, lightweight boots, and fiberfill sleeping bags

Columbia Sportswear Co., P.O. Box 03239, Portland, OR 97203 (503-286-3676): clothing

Eastpak, P.O. Box 471, Haverhill, MA 01830 (617-373-1581): day packs

Gerry Baby Products, 1250 Grant Dr., Denver, CO 80233 (303-457-0926: child carriers

Helly-Hansen, P.O. Box 97031, Redmond, WA 98073 (206-883-4313): clothing and polypropylene underwear

Hi-Tec Sports USA, Inc., 4400 N. Star Way, Modesto, CA 95356 (209-577-1861): lightweight boots

Jansport, Paine Field Industrial Park, Everett, WA 98204 (206-353-0200): day packs and smaller-sized frame packs

Karhu-Titan, 55 Green Mountain Dr. S., Burlington, VT 05401 (802-864-4519): children's cross-country ski packages

Kelty Pack, Inc., 500 Industrial Dr., St. George, UT 84770 (800-423-2320): day packs, smaller-sized frame packs, sleeping bags, and child carriers

Lafuma USA, 3303 Salem Rd., Farmington, GA 30638 (404-769-6627): day packs and child carriers

L. L. Bean, Inc., Casco Street, Freeport, ME 04033 (800-221-4221):

child carriers, day packs, clothing, sleeping bags, and other camping equipment

Log House Designs, HCR-68, P.O. Box 248, Center Conway, NH 03813 (603-535-1894): clothing

Nike, 3900 SW Murray Blvd., Beaverton, OR 97005 (800-344-6453): lightweight boots

The North Face, 999 Harrison St., Berkeley, CA 94719 (415-527-9700): sleeping bags and tents

Recreational Equipment, Inc., (REI), P.O. Box 88125, Seattle, WA 98138 (800-426-4840): day packs, small frame packs, clothing, underwear, lightweight boots, sleeping bags, tents, and other camping and sporting equipment

Patagonia, 259 W. Santa Clara St., P.O. Box 150, Ventura, CA 93002 (805-643-8616): clothing (including pile, bunting, and Synchilla) and Capilene underwear

Slumberjack, 2103 Humboldt St., Los Angeles, CA 90031 (213-225-5905): sleeping bags

Snugli, 12520 Grant Dr., Denver, CO 80233 (303-457-0926): child carriers

Tough Traveler, Ltd., 1012 State St., Schenectady, NY 12307 (800-468-6844): child carriers and day packs

Wigwam Mills, Inc., 3402 Crocker Ave., P.O. Box 818, Sheboygan, WI 53082 (800-558-7760): clothing

Wyoming Woolens, P.O. Box 3127, 890 S. Hwy. 89, Jackson, WY 83001 (307-733-2892): clothing

Government Agencies, Maps, and Park Information

Government agencies are tremendous sources of maps and information for places to hike, ski, canoe, or camp with your family. The following list of addresses and phone numbers covers a wide variety of parks, recreation and wilderness areas, and agency-managed regions appropriate for family recreational use. This listing is by no means complete because there are many recreational areas—too many to adequately detail in a small appendix. A number of agencies, such as the National Park Service, provide free pamphlets and maps upon request. Pamphlet titles are listed under the heading for each agency.

NATIONAL PARK SERVICE

Direct inquiries to the National Park Service at any one of the regions listed below. Be sure to request copies of *The National Parks Camping Guide*, *The National Parks Index*, *The National Parks Lesser Known Areas*, and *The National Park System Map and Guide*. The national office of the Park

Service is National Park Service, United States Department of the Interior, P.O. Box 37127, Washington, D.C. 20013 (202-343-4747).

ALASKA REGION
Alaska
2525 Gambell St., Rm. 107, Anchorage, AK 99503 (907-271-2738)

Parks of Interest: Aniakchak National Monument, Bering Land Bridge National Preserve, Cape Krusenstern National Monument, Denali National Park and Preserve, Gates of the Arctic National Park, Glacier Bay National Park, Katmai National Park, Kenai Fjords National Park, and Klondike Gold Rush National Historic Park.

PACIFIC NORTHWEST REGION
Idaho, Oregon, Washington
83 South King St., Ste. 212, Seattle, WA 98104 (206-442-0170)

Parks of Interest: Craters of the Moon National Monument, Idaho; Crater Lake National Park, Oregon; Coulee Dam National Recreation Area, Mount Rainier National Park, North Cascades National Park, and Olympic National Park, Washington.

WESTERN REGION
Arizona, California, Hawaii, Nevada
450 Golden Gate Ave., P.O. Box 36063, San Francisco, CA 94102 (415-556-0560)

Parks of Interest: Canyon de Chelly National Monument, Casa Grande Ruins National Monument, Chiricahua National Monument, Grand Canyon National Park, Navajo National Monument, Organ Pipe Cactus National Monument, Saguaro National Monument, and Sunset Crater National Monument, Arizona; Channel Islands National Park, Death Valley National Monument, Devils Postpile National Monument, Golden Gate National Recreation Area, Joshua Tree National Monument, Kings Canyon National Park, Lassen Volcanic National Park, Lava Beds National Monument, Muir Woods National Monument, Pinnacles National Monument, Point Reyes National

Seashore, Redwood National Park, Sequoia National Park, Whiskeytown-Shasta Trinity National Recreation Area, and Yosemite National Park, California; Hawaii Volcanoes National Park and Haleakala National Park, Hawaii; Great Basin National Park and Lake Mead National Recreation Area, Nevada.

SOUTHWEST REGION
Arkansas, Louisiana, New Mexico, Oklahoma, Texas
P.O. Box 728, Santa Fe, NM 87504 (505-988-6375)

Parks of Interest: Buffalo National River and Hot Springs National Park, Arkansas; Gulf Island National Seashore, Louisiana; Bandelier National Monument, Chaco Culture National Historical Park, and El Morro National Monument, New Mexico; Chickasaw National Recreation Area, Oklahoma; Amistad Recreation Area, Big Bend National Park, Guadalupe Mountains National Park, Lake Meredith Recreation Area, and Padre Island National Seashore, Texas.

ROCKY MOUNTAIN REGION
Colorado, Montana, North Dakota, South Dakota, Utah, Wyoming
655 Parfet St., P.O. Box 25287, Denver, CO 80225 (303-969-2503)

Parks of Interest: Black Canyon of the Gunnison National Monument, Colorado National Monument, Curecanti National Recreation Area, Great Sand Dunes National Monument, Mesa Verde National Park, and Rocky Mountain National Park, Colorado; Bighorn Canyon National Recreation Area, Montana; Theodore Roosevelt National Park, North Dakota; Badlands National Park and Wind Cave National Park, South Dakota; Arches National Park, Canyon National Park, Canyonlands National Park, Capitol Reef National Park, Cedar Breaks National Monument, Dinosaur National Monument, Glen Canyon National Recreation Area, Hovenweep National Monument, and Zion National Park, Utah; Devils Tower National Monument, Grand Teton National Park, and Yellowstone National Park, Wyoming.

Wilderness with Children

MIDWEST REGION

Illinois, Indiana, Iowa, Kansas, Michigan, Minnesota, Missouri, Nebraska, Ohio, Wisconsin
1709 Jackson St., Omaha, NE 68102 (402-221-3477)

Parks of Interest: Indiana Dunes National Lakeshore, Indiana; Effigy Mounds National Monument, Iowa; Isle Royal National Park, Pictured Rocks National Lakeshore, and Sleeping Bear Dunes National Lakeshore, Michigan; Grand Portage National Monument, Pipestone National Monument, and Voyageurs National Park, Minnesota; George Washington Carver National Monument and Ozark National Scenic Riverways, Missouri; Agate Fossil Beds National Monument and Scotts Bluff National Monument, Nebraska; Apostle Island National Lakeshore, Wisconsin.

SOUTHEAST REGION

Alabama, Florida, Georgia, Kentucky, Mississippi, North Carolina, South Carolina, Tennessee
75 Spring St., SW, Atlanta, GA 30303 (404-331-5187)

Parks of Interest: Russell Cave National Monument, Alabama; Biscayne National Park, Everglades National Park, Fort Jefferson National Monument, and Gulf Islands National Seashore, Florida; Chickamauga and Chattanooga National Military Park and Cumberland Island National Seashore, Georgia; Cumberland Gap National Historic Park and Mammoth Cave National Park, Kentucky; Natchez Trace Parkway, Mississippi; Blue Ridge Parkway, Cape Hatteras National Seashore, and Cape Lookout National Seashore, North Carolina; Big South Fork National River and Recreation Area and Great Smoky Mountains National Park, Tennessee.

MID-ATLANTIC REGION

Delaware, Maryland, Pennsylvania, Virginia, West Virginia
143 S. Third St., Philadelphia, PA 19106 (215-597-3678)

Parks of Interest: Antietam National Battlefield, Assateague Island National Seashore, Catoctin Mountain Park, Chesapeake and Ohio Canal National Historical Park, and Greenbelt Park, Maryland; Delaware Water Gap National Recreation Area, Fort Necessity

Appendix V

National Battlefield, and Gettysburg National Military Park, Pennsylvania; Prince William Forest Park and Shenandoah National Park, Virginia.

NORTH ATLANTIC REGION
Connecticut, Maine, Massachusetts, New Hampshire, New Jersey, New York, Rhode Island, Vermont
15 State St., Boston, MA 02109 (617-565-8888)

Parks of Interest: Acadia National Park, Maine; Fire Island National Seashore, New York.

UNITED STATES FOREST SERVICE

When requesting information from the Forest Service you will receive fast printouts on policies and camping locations. Ask for *A Guide to Your National Forest*, a large map that details all the facilities operated by the agency.

Address your requests to the U.S. Forest Service at any of the addresses listed below.

ALASKA
709 W. Ninth St., P.O. Box 21628, Juneau, AK 99802 (907-586-8863)

OREGON AND WASHINGTON
319 Southwest Pine St., P.O. Box 3623, Portland, OR 97208 (503-221-2877)

CALIFORNIA
630 Sansome St., San Francisco, CA 94111 (415-556-0122)

ARIZONA AND NEW MEXICO
517 Gold Ave., SW, Albuquerque, NM 87102 (505-842-3292)

IDAHO, NEVADA, UTAH, AND PARTS OF WYOMING
324 25th St., Ogden, UT 84401 (801-625-5354)

COLORADO, NEBRASKA, SOUTH DAKOTA, AND PARTS OF
WYOMING
11177 W. Eighth Ave., P.O. Box 25127, Lakewood, CO 80225 (303-236-
9431)

MONTANA AND PARTS OF IDAHO
200 E. Broadway St., P.O. Box 7669, Missoula, MT 59807 (406-329-3511)

ALABAMA, ARKANSAS, FLORIDA, GEORGIA, KENTUCKY, LOUISIANA,
MISSISSIPPI, NORTH CAROLINA, SOUTH CAROLINA, TENNESSEE,
TEXAS, AND VIRGINIA
1720 Peachtree Rd., NW, Atlanta, GA 30367 (404-347-4191)

ILLINOIS, INDIANA, OHIO, MICHIGAN, MINNESOTA, MISSOURI,
NEW HAMPSHIRE, MAINE, PENNSYLVANIA, VERMONT, WEST
VIRGINIA, AND WISCONSIN
310 W. Wisconsin Ave., Rm. 500, Milwaukee, WI 53203 (414-291-3693)

UNITED STATES BUREAU OF LAND MANAGEMENT

Bureau of Land Management (BLM) land is public, and most of it is located in the western states, often abutting Forest Service land. Much of the land is open to a variety of recreational uses, including wilderness camping. Each regional office will send you a map, which lists sites and addresses for each BLM facility. Request the *Recreation Guide to BLM Public Lands*. In addition, request information about Back Country Byways, a network of secondary roads, dirt roads, and ATV or mountain-bike-use trails available to the public through BLM lands. Address your requests to any of the addresses below. The national office of the BLM is United States Bureau of Land Management, 1849 C St. NW, MIB 5600, Washington, D.C. 20240 (202-208-5717).

ALASKA
701 C St., P.O. Box 13, Anchorage, AK 99513 (907-217-5555)

ARIZONA
P.O. Box 16563, Phoenix, AZ 85011 (602-241-5504)

CALIFORNIA
2800 Cottage Way, Rm. E-2841, Sacramento, CA 95825 (916-978-4746)

COLORADO
2850 Youngfield St., Lakewood, CO 80215 (303-294-7090)

IDAHO
3380 Americana Terrace, Boise, ID 83706 (208-334-1770)

MONTANA, NORTH DAKOTA, SOUTH DAKOTA
P.O. Box 36800, Billings, MT 59107 (406-657-6561)

NEVADA
850 Harvard Way, P.O. Box 12000, Reno, NV 89520 (702-784-5311)

NEW MEXICO, OKLAHOMA, KANSAS, TEXAS
P.O. Box 1449, Santa Fe, NM 87504 (505-988-6316)

OREGON, WASHINGTON
825 Northeast Multinomah St., P.O. Box 2965, Portland, OR 97208 (503-231-6274)

UTAH
324 South State St., Salt Lake City, UT 84111 (801-524-3146)

WYOMING, NEBRASKA
2515 Warren Ave., P.O. Box 1828, Cheyenne, WY 82003 (307-772-2111)

UNITED STATES ARMY CORPS OF ENGINEERS

The U.S. Army Corps of Engineers does more than build dams and roads, really! They provide a tremendous number of recreational areas, which are open to camping on a first come basis. Many of these areas also offer boating opportunities. Request maps of all sites by writing the main office, or request specific-site information by writing the district or division office managing that area. Address all requests to the U.S. Army Corps of Engineers. The main office is U.S. Army Corps of Engineers, 20 Massachusetts Ave., Washington, D.C. 20314 (202-272-0247).

LOWER MISSISSIPPI VALLEY
P.O. Box 80, Vicksburg, MS 39180 (601-634-5885)

MISSOURI RIVER
P.O. Box 103, Downtown Station, Omaha, NE 68101 (402-221-7284)

NEW ENGLAND
424 Trapelo Rd., Waltham, MA 02254 (617-647-8305)

NORTH ATLANTIC
90 Church St., New York, NY 10007 (212-264-7534)

NORTH CENTRAL
536 South Clark St., Chicago, IL 60605 (312-353-7762)

NORTH PACIFIC
P.O. Box 2870, Portland, OR 97208 (503-326-4087)

OHIO RIVER
P.O. Box 1159, Cincinnati, OH 45201 (513-684-3192)

SOUTH ATLANTIC
77 Forsythe St., SW, Rm. 313, Atlanta, GA 30335 (404-331-6746)

SOUTH PACIFIC
630 Samsome St., Rm. 1216, San Francisco, CA 94111 (415-705-1443)

SOUTHWESTERN
1114 Commerce St., Dallas, TX 75242 (214-767-2435)

UNITED STATES FISH AND WILDLIFE SERVICE

There are very few camping opportunities at U.S. Fish and Wildlife areas, but there are a great number of other recreational possibilities. Many of the preserves provide access to boating, bicycling, hiking, hunting, and fishing. Request the map *National Wildlife Refuges: A Visitor's Guide*. The main office of the service is United States Fish and Wildlife Service, Washington, D.C. 20240 (202-343-4311).

CANADIAN PROVINCIAL TOURISM OFFICES

Canada offers some of the most wonderful and remote parks in North America. Camping, boating, and other recreational opportunities abound. When making your travel inquiries, be sure to specifically request camping, boating, biking, and other wilderness-oriented and related information.

ALBERTA
Travel Alberta, 10025 Jasper Ave., 15th Fl., Edmonton, AB T5J 3Z3 Canada (800-661-8888)

BRITISH COLUMBIA
Ministry of Tourism, Recreation, and Culture, Parliament Bldgs., Victoria, BC V8V 1X4 Canada (800-663-6000)

MANITOBA
Travel Manitoba, Dept. 6020, 155 Carlton St., 7th Fl., Winnipeg, MB R3C 3H8 Canada (800-665-0040)

NEW BRUNSWICK
Tourism, Recreation, and Heritage, Casier Postal, P.O. Box 12345, Fredericton, NB E3B 5C3 Canada (800-561-0123)

NEWFOUNDLAND/LABRADOR
Department of Development and Tourism, P.O. Box 2016, Sta. A, St. John's, NE A1C 5R8 Canada (800-563-6353)

NOVA SCOTIA
Department of Tourism, P.O. Box 130, Halifax, NS B3J 2M7 Canada (800-341-6096)

NORTHWEST TERRITORIES
Travel Arctic, Government of the Northwest Territories, Yellowknife, NWT X1A 2L9 Canada (800-661-0788)

ONTARIO
Ministry of Tourism and Recreation, Queen's Park, Toronto, ON M7A 2E5 Canada (800-268-3735)

PRINCE EDWARD ISLAND
Department of Tourism and Parks, Visitor Services, P.O. Box 940, Charlottetown, PEI C1A 7M5 Canada (800-561-0123)

QUEBEC
Tourisme Quebec, P.O. Box 20,000, Quebec City, PQ G1K 7X2 Canada (800-443-7000)

SASKATCHEWAN
Tourism Saskatchewan, 1919 Saskatchewan Dr., Regina, SK S4P 3V7 Canada (800-667-7191)

YUKON TERRITORY
Tourism Yukon, P.O. Box 2703, Whitehorse, YK Y1A 2C6 Canada (403-667-5340)